Praise for *Reading the Bible, Missing the Gospel*

Hebrews 3:3 says, "Jesus has been counted worthy of more glory than Moses—as much more glory as the builder of a house has more honor than the house itself." Jesus' story is on every page of the Bible. His love, His power, and His victory show up everywhere. People miss this if we think the star of the Bible's story is ourselves. When we do this, we look for self-glory or self-affirmation, or complain about our role in God's story. Both thoughts miss Jesus and the greatness He alone deserves. And both thoughts lead us to misapply the Bible in our lives. Ben, thank you for writing a book that reminds us not to be amazed by the house itself but to be amazed by the builder of the house. That's Jesus.

SHAUN ALEXANDER, 2005 NFL MVP; author; entrepreneur; disciple of Jesus

I'm sorry to tell you this, but the book you're holding in your hands right now is going to challenge some of your longest-held beliefs. In the best possible way. Calling readers back to Scripture, *Reading the Bible, Missing the Gospel* invites us to discover the "good news" afresh and to learn how God's vision will always be bigger and better than what we settle for.

HANNAH ANDERSON, author of *All That's Good: Recovering the Lost Art of Discernment*

Deconstruction can be a fruitful endeavor. Ben Connelly not only helps us to deconstruct how we read the Bible, but more importantly, he helps us to reconstruct the way that we read the Bible, in and through the living Word. The good news is that Scripture reads us more accurately than we read it and reveals to us our need of the Father who loves us, the Son who gives us grace, and the Spirit who empowers us to follow Christ.

JR WOODWARD, National Director, The V3 Movement; author, *Creating a Missional Culture*; coauthor, *The Church as Movement*

Ben Connelly brings years of experience as an equipper of church planters alongside his own work as a planter to the crucial question, "What is the gospel?" He writes with biblical depth, the wisdom of experience and the heart of a disciple-maker. I highly recommend careful study for the sake of the kingdom of Jesus.

GERRY BRESHEARS, Professor of Theology, Western Seminary, Portland

Please read this book about THE BOOK! For a follower of Jesus, reading and knowing the Bible is everything since it is the objective source of our faith. Sadly, few read it and fewer study it, and yet when many do, they do so often studying some book or subject in the Bible disconnected from the greater whole of God's story and the gospel. Recently, I've read a couple of books on reading books—which has tremendously helped me. This book will have a profound impact on how you read the Bible and the lens you see it through.

BOB ROBERTS JR., Founder, Glocal.net and Multi-Faith Neighbors Network; Senior Global Pastor, Northwood Church

Far too many people have been reading the Bible visually impaired, missing the beauty of the expansive landscape of the good news of Jesus Christ. Sadly, they either burden themselves with a crushing load of guilt, shame, or performance-driven expectations, or they walk away never having taken in the life-giving beauty of Jesus when they consider key themes of Scripture. Ben's work reveals the reason so many remain blind to the beauty, while providing a means to begin seeing clearly the treasures of Jesus Christ found in every page of the Bible.

JEFF VANDERSTELT, Executive Director of Saturate and author of *Saturate, Gospel Fluency,* and *Making Space*

Among the morass of books written to help us read the Bible, this one stands out. Its prose is clear, and illustrations are compelling. It helpfully exposes common errors in Bible reading and guides readers into more faithful interpretation. It also avoids complicated hermeneutical discussions while handing the reader the ultimate interpretive lens—the gospel of Jesus Christ. Here is a theologically rich yet eminently practical way to read the Bible *with* Jesus!

JONATHAN DODSON, Lead Pastor, City Life Church; author, *Gospel-Centered Discipleship* and *The Unwavering Pastor*

Reading the Bible, Missing the Gospel is a wonderful resource to help believers see the Scriptures as they are meant to be seen—as one unified story that points to Jesus, our source of life. Ben Connelly helps us see that this vision correction of a "gospel lens" of reading the Bible brings the pages of Scriptures to life! No longer is the Bible simply a book of rules, or quick bits of encouragement, or random "truths" about God, but it is the story of God in which Jesus is the Hero and we are joy-filled participants. If you're looking to better understand the relevance of the Bible and the person of Jesus for everyday life, get this book. It is challenging yet winsome, theological yet accessible—a great addition to the bookshelves of clergy and laity alike.

DOUG LOGAN JR., President of Grimké Seminary; Vice President for Advancement of the Acts 29 Network; author of *On the Block: Developing a Biblical Picture for Missional Engagement*

Practical, theologically deep, and clarifying, this book will challenge your entire approach to the Bible if you—like so many (including me)—just find yourself reading it all wrong sometimes. Ben is a gift to the church in today's climate, where we have more Bibles than ever but not always a clear understanding of what it is actually all about. Get this book, and give it to a friend or three!

MARK CLARK, Teaching Pastor, Bayside Church (CA); Founding Pastor, Village Church (BC)

It is not enough to read the Bible. One must know how to read the Bible rightly. With pastoral care and a humorous heart, Ben speaks to each of us, gently showing us where we have misstepped in our reading, both culturally and religiously. He does not, however, abandon us. Instead, he points us hopefully toward a brighter and more holistic path. He leads us further up and further into the great Story, making us better readers and, in the end, better participants in remaking the world. Highly recommended.

STEVE BEZNER, Senior Pastor, Houston Northwest Church; adjunct instructor, Truett Theological Seminary, Baylor University

READING THE BIBLE

MISSING THE GOSPEL

RECOVERING FROM (SHOCKINGLY COMMON) WAYS WE GET THE BIBLE WRONG IN OUR EVERYDAY LIVES

BEN CONNELLY

MOODY PUBLISHERS

CHICAGO

Unless otherwise indicated, Scripture quotations are from the ESV® Bible (The Holy Bible, English Standard Version®), Copyright © 2001 by Crossway, a publishing ministry of Good News Publishers. Used by permission. All rights reserved.

Scripture quotations marked (NIV) are taken from the Holy Bible, New International Version®, NIV®. Copyright © 1973, 1978, 1984, 2011 by Biblica, Inc.™ Used by permission of Zondervan. All rights reserved worldwide. www.zondervan.com The "NIV" and "New International Version" are trademarks registered in the United States Patent and Trademark Office by Biblica, Inc.™

Scripture quotations marked MSG are taken from THE MESSAGE, copyright © 1993, 2002, 2018 by Eugene H. Peterson. Used by permission of NavPress, represented by Tyndale House Publishers. All rights reserved.

Scripture quotations marked (GNT) are from the Good News Translation in Today's English Version- Second Edition Copyright © 1992 by American Bible Society. Used by Permission.

All emphasis in Scripture has been added.

Published in association with the literary agency of The Gates Group.

Edited by Pamela J. Pugh
Cover and interior design: Erik M. Peterson
Cover illustration of glasses copyright © 2018 by cveiv / iStock Photos (1003883462). All rights reserved.

Library of Congress Cataloging-in-Publication Data

Names: Connelly, Ben (Pastor), author.
Title: Reading the Bible, missing the Gospel : recovering from (shockingly common) ways we get the Bible wrong in our everyday lives / Ben Connelly.
Description: Chicago : Moody Publishers, 2022. | Includes bibliographical references. | Summary: "In Reading the Bible, Missing the Gospel, pastor and author Ben Connelly shows us how to recover God's original intentions in light of the story of redemption. Connelly helps us celebrate and understand how Jesus' life, death, and resurrection are truly good news for the tangible situations in our everyday lives. Biblical misunderstandings can lead to a small view of God-but truth overturns that. It expands our hearts for God and enables us to truly love others!"-- Provided by publisher.
Identifiers: LCCN 2022007919 (print) | LCCN 2022007920 (ebook) | ISBN 9780802428493 (paperback) | ISBN 9780802475435 (ebook)
Subjects: LCSH: Bible--Criticism, interpretation, etc.
Classification: LCC BS511.3 .C6545 2022 (print) | LCC BS511.3 (ebook) | DDC 220.6--dc23/eng/20220506
LC record available at https://lccn.loc.gov/2022007919
LC ebook record available at https://lccn.loc.gov/2022007920

Originally delivered by fleets of horse-drawn wagons, the affordable paperbacks from D. L. Moody's publishing house resourced the church and served everyday people. Now, after more than 125 years of publishing and ministry, Moody Publishers' mission remains the same— even if our delivery systems have changed a bit. For more information on other books (and resources) created from a biblical perspective, go to www.moodypublishers.com or write to:

Moody Publishers
820 N. LaSalle Boulevard
Chicago, IL 60610

3 5 7 9 10 8 6 4 2

Printed in the United States of America

To my parents, Dennis and Becky—
for displaying the good news of Jesus consistently,
and for never "settling" in your pursuit of God
and His truth in your everyday lives.

CONTENTS

FOREWORD

In John 8, we find a fascinating exchange between Jesus and some religious leaders that reveals a lot about the nature of belief and about the nature of Jesus Himself. Now, the four gospels record numerous run-ins with the theological-industrial complex of the day, but in John 8:48–59, the leaders come out swinging. They basically accuse Jesus of being demon-possessed.

Jesus, of course, denies the charge. And then He begins to thwart their presumed authority by asserting His own—not just as a spiritual guru or as a theologian or even as a pillar of moral example, but as the center of the God-blessed universe. He tells them, first of all, that God is invested in Jesus' glory. He tells them that if they believe in His word, they won't die. He tells them that Abraham envisioned His ministry. And He tells them, in fact, that before Abraham *was*, Jesus *is*.

This is a series of staggering claims all neatly stacked on top of one another, and what they amount to is a claim of divine authority, of divine self-revelation. Jesus is obviously claiming to be God.

Naturally, the leaders are unsettled by this. In their mind, Jesus is blaspheming. So they take up stones to execute Him.

The spiritual import of this scene should be revealing to everyone who reads it. Jesus has revealed the vital, life-giving truth about Himself, and He is rejected. More than that, He is despised. And the religious leaders want to kill Him. And then something extraordinary—if we have the eyes to see it—happens. In verse 59, we read that as they picked up stones to throw at Him, "Jesus hid himself and went out of the temple."

What do you suppose that means, He "hid himself"?

Did Jesus run away? Did He jump behind a nearby pillar? Did He pull one of those "Hey look over there, guys!" ruses and hide when they were distracted?

It is difficult to say, but this looks like it could be a miraculous obscuring. It's possible that Jesus became, effectively, invisible. There is a similar incident in Luke 4 where an angry crowd has pushed Jesus to the edge of a cliff to throw Him off, and He just walks right through them. Ever wonder how He managed that?

But I don't think this is just some neat trick. Whether Jesus literally hid Himself behind something in order to sneak away or He supernaturally veiled himself in some way, the point either way is heartbreaking. *They can't see Him.*

The theological importance of this reality is perhaps the primary point of the entire scene. Disbelief blinds us. These guys are looking right at Jesus, but somehow, they cannot see Him for who He truly is.

The worst thing that can ever happen to us is to be closed off to the glory of Christ. The worst thing that can ever happen to us is to reject Jesus and have His glory hidden from us. Because there is nothing better than to behold the glory of Jesus. His glory alone is ultimately satisfying and eternally saving.

And a similar danger is one that even genuine believers in Jesus sometimes face. One of the worst things about a lot of folks' experience of church is that they go a lot of years reading their Bibles and not really seeing Jesus—even when they're reading *about* Him. It's possible to look at Jesus and not *see* Him.

I had been a Christian a long time and had been reading my Bible for more than two decades before I realized I was missing the point of the whole thing. The point of the whole thing is Jesus.

Our Lord tells us this over and over again in His earthly ministry. He reframes all the Scriptures around Himself. There in John 8, He tells the "Bible teachers" that if they really believed in Abraham, they would believe in Him, because Abraham himself is pointing to Jesus.

Once I realized the whole Bible was pointing me toward and culminating in the glory of Christ, it was like putting on glasses for the first time. Everything became so much clearer, so much more resonant. Ben Connelly uses that analogy in the opening of his fine book on this subject too. And this is why I'm grateful for this unique contribution to the field of what we formally call "biblical theology." Ben painstakingly, with a pastoral heart and a Bible-tuned ear, clears the air for us, dismantling misconceptions and reframing our vision of the Scriptures back to their central and exhilarating point—the glory of Jesus.

Too many of us read the Bible and miss Jesus, even if we're looking at Him. So read slowly. Let Ben challenge you. Even if you find yourself disagreeing with some of his specific conclusions, be grateful for the wrestling match he's setting you up for. It's impossible to come to grips with Jesus and walk away unchanged. You may end up with a limp, but the blessing will be worth it!

As too many even in today's so-called gospel-centered movement seem to have drifted away from a galvanizing grace or moved on to matters assumed more interesting, we need ever-new examinations of our vision and reminders to upgrade our interpretive lenses. *Reading the Bible, Missing the Gospel* is one such examination and reminder. And it's a joyous one, at that.

JARED C. WILSON
Midwestern Seminary

"You search the Scriptures because you think that in them you have eternal life; and it is they that bear witness about me, yet you refuse to come to me that you may have life."

JOHN 5:39–40

EYE
SURGERY

"WE'LL NEED TO DO SURGERY TO CORRECT HIS VISION."

My heart sank as I looked from the doctor to my wife, Jess, to Travis, our not-even-one-year-old son. Several thoughts swirled in a split second: *Eye surgery? My baby son will be under anesthesia! He only has two eyes—what if something goes wrong? I think I'd rather lose any other part of my body than my eyes.*

Through the immediate spiral of fear and concern, my only momentary consolation—which, looking back now, wasn't much—was that if something went terribly wrong, Travis would still be able to see with his other eye.

But that comforting thought was dashed as the doctor continued. "We'll need to operate on both eyes . . ." More swirling thoughts interrupted him: *No . . . okay, this guy does this all the time . . . but what if my kid's the one he messes up? Should we wait on the surgery?* But those thoughts too were suddenly silenced by the doctor's terrifying conclusion: "And if we don't do this soon, his brain will stop registering impulses from this eye, and it will stop working." *Well, okay then.*

We had known of Travis's lazy eye for several months. Of course, there's a fancy technical term for the condition, but the bottom line is that his misaligned eyes impacted his vision and balance, and one day his brain would eventually "turn off" the bad eye. We tried covering his good eye with patches to strengthen the weaker one. While the patches led to some cute photographs, they didn't work. We tried exercises, which also didn't work.

His inability to see clearly was causing developmental issues. Travis wasn't able to focus on things he was looking at. His balance was off; he couldn't even really sit up for more than a few seconds. So, after talking, praying, and following the doctor's wisdom, Jess and I took our baby son in for eye surgery.

The results? They were amazing. And immediate!

There were stunningly few aftereffects. No more patches, no lasting surgical marks. And Travis did not seem to be in an iota of pain. It was as if no operation had taken place! More surprisingly, it was as if Travis had never had a lazy eye in the first place. Within a couple days of getting home, he was sitting up. We could see him able to focus on things—*he could fully see for the first time.* Having spent his whole albeit short up-to-that-point life unable to see clearly, in an instant he could. It was truly amazing to watch, and while we've had to do one follow-up operation, we are grateful to God and Dr. Norman that Travis's sight continues to be clear. As I write this, he's a happy, coordinated, clear-eyed elementary-aged boy, and you'd never know he once had a problem.

(Except that now his dad wrote about it in a book . . . *ugh, dads.*)

A BLURRY VIEW OF THE BIBLE

Several times as I've thought about Travis's surgery, a scene from Jesus' life has come to mind. As recorded in Mark's gospel, Jesus enters Bethsaida, a fishing village at the mouth of the Jordan River:

> Some people brought to [Jesus] a blind man and begged him to touch him. And he took the blind man by the hand and led him out of the village, and when he had spit on his eyes and laid his hands on him, he asked him, "Do you see anything?" And he looked up and said, "I see people, but they look like trees, walking." Then Jesus laid his hands on his eyes again; and he opened his eyes, his sight was restored, and he saw everything clearly. (Mark 8:22–25)

Travis's story is different, but in his early months his sight was similarly foggy. He could see proverbial "trees": something like shadowy shapes and blurry colors filled his mind rather than the precision and focus most of us are used to. Then suddenly, "he saw everything clearly." Any of us with strong lens prescriptions can perhaps relate: we know the frustration and annoyance of a fuzzy and unclear world. And we also know the immediate correction and relief of popping in contacts or putting on eyeglasses. Seeing clearly is a blessing, sure, but it's also essential for much of life! From night driving, to watching a game or show from the cheap seats, to activities in our jobs or schools, to nearly everything else we give time to, we *must* see clearly.

The same is true when we read the Bible: to read it right, we need to see clearly. We don't just need to read clearly for the sake of gaining knowledge, but because the Bible is from God and informs every aspect of our whole life. But even if we don't realize it, many earnest followers of Jesus see the words of the Bible through the wrong lens. Several of us have even been *taught* to see the Bible through the wrong lens. We've trusted our spiritual ophthalmologists, if you will—our pastors, teachers, and authors—but have, at times, been sent home with the wrong prescription.

Perhaps you too have felt confused, frustrated, overwhelmed, or burdened at times by the Bible. What if it's because we read the Bible wrong?

Many "wrong lenses" have been prescribed to many followers of Jesus over the years, and the danger is greater than just giving us a headache: these wrong lenses lead us to miss the very heart of the Bible altogether and thus misinform various aspects of our walk with God, our relationships with others, and our everyday lives. Like you, I've sat in various Bible studies over the years. No matter the setting, church, or group makeup, it's not uncommon to hear similar phrases at some point when discussing the Bible's various verses, commands, and stories: "I just don't get this." "Surely God can't actually mean that." "That worked back then, but not today." "There's no way I could measure up."

Perhaps you too have felt confused, frustrated, overwhelmed, or burdened at times by the Bible—and felt tension because you also remember that Jesus said His "burden is light" and "where the Spirit of the Lord is, there is freedom" (Matt. 11:30; 2 Cor. 3:17). What if the tension exists because we read the Bible wrong? Over the coming pages, together we'll recover a better vision of the Bible. We'll rediscover God's intent, long lost to many of us. And we'll return to Jesus' life, death, resurrection, and reign as the reality that brings clarity, color, and understanding to the whole Bible, which shapes our everyday lives.

To that end, think of the first three chapters of this book as a trip to the eye doctor: we'll look at various common-but-poor lenses through which we're often taught to read the Bible. We'll see the danger of reading the Bible through these lenses, and why we must trade up to better lenses. And we'll see from the Bible how God intends for us to read the Bible and how it impacts our lives—perhaps in ways that are different than we've previously known.

The key to engaging God's message is shockingly simple—but also missed shockingly often.

But like getting a new pair of glasses, this "new" lens (which is actually "ancient," as it's what God originally intended) will take some getting used to. So, while the first three chapters reshape our view of the Bible, the rest of the book is a series of examples. We'll look at a few well-known verses, commands, and stories, and see how each is commonly misunderstood or mistaught based on our wrong lenses. Then we'll see each through the right lens of Jesus' life, death, resurrection, and reign—and how the gospel informs a right, better, truer understanding of that command or story. And as we rediscover the true heart of God's message, we'll course-correct, turning from wrong understanding to the massive difference right understanding makes in our everyday lives.

READING THE BIBLE, MISSING THE GOSPEL

Get ready; we will keep the ophthalmology metaphor up for a while (even though I had to use autocorrect *every single time* I typed the word!). I'm no doctor, but I have been a local church pastor for over twenty years, and also get to train church leaders around the world through my work with The Equipping Group. In hundreds of discussions with church staff, group leaders, seminary and university students, small groups, and counseling sessions, I've seen over and over moments like the one where an ophthalmologist drops that final lens into place during an eye test, where you gasp and say breathlessly, "That's it!" That's what I pray happens for you, dear reader, throughout the coming pages: as we click through different lenses ("one or two? one or two?"), I hope we see the difference the Bible makes in our understanding of God and how that shapes our lives, better than we ever have.

Jesus gives us that right lens—the one that helps the Bible snap into focus and unlocks the door to God's true message and its implication for our lives—in another scene from His life. This one is in John's gospel and is a rebuke from Jesus to the religious leaders of His day. They read their Scriptures, which is our Old Testament, through wrong lenses. But as is similar to our experience today, God's "voice you have never heard, his form you have never seen, and you do not have his word abiding in you, for you do not believe the one whom he has sent. *You search the Scriptures because you think that in them you have eternal life; and it is they that bear witness about me, yet you refuse to come to me that you may have life*" (John 5:37–40).

Essentially, Jesus says that even the most religious people of His day read the Bible through the wrong lens. These were Jewish leaders, whose role was to represent God to the rest of God's people; to teach God's word and ways. But Jesus' claim was that they never actually heard the voice of God. So, though they were earnest and religious, they missed the point! These leaders spent hours studying their scrolls—but for all the time they stared at the words, Jesus says they never saw the greatest truth those words point to: Himself, the Messiah, the One God sent to fulfill each of His promises.

It is both shocking and common how much these first-century Jewish leaders' issues still pervade today's religious leaders, churches, and everyday followers of Jesus. If they truly understood God's promises, they would recognize Jesus as the fulfillment of each one. If they grasped the words of the prophets, they'd see Jesus as the culmination of all prophecy. If the words of Scripture shone a light on their own hearts, they would realize the hypocrisy and brokenness of their own life in contrast to Jesus' perfection. And for all their yearning for a Messiah, they would recognize Jesus as the "one [God] sent." And so would we.

The sobering (terrifying?) conclusion in Jesus' rebuke is that the leaders wrongly "search the Scriptures because you think that in *them* you have eternal life." Do we do the same, as we look to the Bible for recommendations and fixes, and hope that it's convicting enough to lead us to change ourselves? As we'll see, the words of the Bible—as helpful and vital as they are for followers of Jesus—are *not* themselves the source of life.

What is Jesus' remedy? Life is found *in Him*! By His exemplary life, sacrificial death, miraculous resurrection, and kingdom reign, Jesus offers us true, full *life*, both today and for eternity. That's the gospel, the "good news" that changes every aspect of life, but that we often miss when we read the Bible.

It's increasingly common to hear that every story and command in the Bible points to Jesus and the gospel. Yes and amen! But what's still often missed is *how* the gospel informs the Bible's many verses, commands, and stories, and gives a right view of how the Bible shapes our everyday lives: How does the gospel inform our understanding of the Old Testament's 613 commands? How is Jesus a better example to follow than Paul, David, Esther, or Peter—and what happens when we can't follow His example? How do God's holiness and grace both meet us as we read Paul's New Testament letters? How does the gospel inform the ways we try to apply the Bible to our lives?

These are the kind of answers we're pursuing together over the coming pages. That's the correction we need from getting the Bible wrong in our everyday lives. That's the new (ancient) lens we—like the leaders in John 5—often miss as we read the Bible. It's that lens alone that gives us true, deep, abiding life. And it's that lens we will rediscover together in the coming pages.

If you're ready for a better vision of God's Word for your life, then ask God—the Great Physician who gives sight to the blind—to help us see Him better. Then turn the page, leave the proverbial waiting room, and "come on back."

See missingthegospel.com for exercises and additional resources, to help you practice and go deeper into the chapters and theme of this book.

PART 1

A
SPIRITUAL
EYE
EXAM

or
Discovering a
New (Ancient) Lens
for the Bible

"Therefore I testify to you this day that I am innocent of the blood of all, for I did not shrink from declaring to you the whole counsel of God."

ACTS 20:26–27

CHAPTER 1

SYMPTOMS: READING THE BIBLE, WRONG

"YOU CAN'T READ A BOOK THAT WAY!"

Charlotte, my oldest kiddo, had avoided J. K. Rowling's Harry Potter series for most of her elementary years—maybe just because of the overabundance of "Harrys and Hermiones" who filled her school's annual storybook parade. But over the summer before fourth grade, her tune changed, and she devoured all seven books and 4,100-plus pages in three months. (She'd say she also read the script of the Broadway play too, but I don't think that counts.) This started a domino effect, and while we went slower with our two younger kids—the books get dark!—Harry and Co. became the Connellys' constant companions over the following years.

Sometimes after that first summer, I saw Charlotte with one of the series paperbacks in hand, while the next day she had a different one. She's a fast reader, but that seemed *really* quick. After a few times, I asked her how she was reading so quickly. "Oh," she explained, laughing at my obvious ignorance. "I'm not reading the whole book. I just go back and read the parts I like." Now, as a writer, a lover of good stories, and a guy who appreciates the craft of literature, her comment birthed immediate indignation in me: "You can't read a book that way!" That was my first, sudden thought: the series is one long but unified story, meant to be read as such. It has ups and downs, twists and turns, and heroes, each perfectly crafted and painstakingly placed by the author.

On the heels of that first thought was a second startling realization: Most followers of Jesus read the Bible the way Charlotte reads Harry Potter. We just go back and read the parts we like, or jump to verses we feel might apply to something in our lives today. We reread the stories we know, memorize a few verses that'll be inspirational, or ignore parts that are confusing.

In things like this, we miss large and valuable parts of the Bible, even if they *are* parts we don't like or understand. We might not ever discover new verses that "apply to my life today," as we like to say, because we never come across them! More deeply, though, we miss the long-but-unified story with its ups and downs, twists and turns, and true hero; each perfectly inspired by God and scribed by an intentional, human author.

This chapter looks at symptoms, defining the poor lenses we approach the Bible with. We're trying to discover why God's people miss the heart of God's message as we read God's Word; why we get the Bible wrong in our everyday lives. As good spiritual ophthalmologists, we find two symptoms that lead us to the next chapter's diagnosis. First, statistically, Christians don't read the Bible all that much! Second, when we do read it, we do so in little bits. Chapter 2 shows how dangerous these symptoms are, but for now, as we look at each symptom, be honest: Are either of them true of you?

"FOND OF THE BIBLE" . . . WITHOUT READING IT

The Bible has been increasingly accessible to followers of Jesus, especially since the invention of the printing press. Its accessibility has increased throughout history, many editions now landing on our pocket-sized mobile devices. As literacy has also increased over history, countless of us across the world have the opportunity to access the Bible on our own terms, in our own languages, to read or listen whenever we want. However, we also have opportunities of going to the gym, declining dessert, and *not* clicking "watch next episode" when it's pushing midnight. But do we take them?

Media researcher Amy Watson reports that in 2021, only 11 percent of the over three thousand Christians surveyed read their Bible "every day," and 9 percent "several times a week." While 46 percent of Christians read the Bible between "less than once a year" and "once a week," she reports that 29 percent of respondents read their Bible "never."[1]

The Bible, Limited

Similarly, a Lifeway survey a few years before—whose tongue-in-cheek title is telling: "Americans Are Fond of the Bible, Don't Actually Read It"—reports that, of the thousand Americans surveyed who *do* read their Bible, only "four in 10 say it's a book worth reading over and over, while 13 percent say it's worth reading once. Twenty-two percent prefer referencing the Bible on an as-needed basis. Five percent say the Bible is a book not worth reading at all, while 19 percent are not sure."[2]

So, as we can see, the first symptom for missing the gospel

when reading the Bible is that statistically, not even many of us bona fide, self-proclaiming followers of Jesus read the Bible very often! Obviously since you've picked up this book you have some affection, or at least a curiosity, around this topic of Bible reading, and perhaps these stats surprise you. Or maybe you fit within one of those categories.

But to let you off the hook a bit, the blame isn't all on you. While Christian faith is personal, it is not individualistic. Every relationship with God exists in one part of the world, at one point in history, and in a church or religious culture whose expectations become the tide we naturally ride. So, like other cultural norms—for example, what's the appropriate if unspoken dress code for your church's gatherings?—the way we engage the Bible is often shaped by our church's culture. But surely our churches form God's people to engage God's Word well and regularly, right? *Crickets . . .*

> Like other cultural norms, the amount and way we engage the Bible is often shaped by our church's culture.

Well, maybe not. Some churches promote Bible reading plans in which all or parts of the Old or New Testaments are covered within a few years. Some have classes like Bible 101, or small groups where a Scripture passage can be discussed among peers. But a passage of Scripture is often referenced the way many churches approach the Bible: the Sermon Almighty.

I've served in local churches for more than twenty years and have crafted and delivered over a thousand sermons. I believe in the gathered church; I believe teaching is a vital and biblical aspect of discipleship and worship; and I believe teaching can look different across churches and cultures. But I also know that no matter the tradition, churches can misinform—or mis-form—God's people in their engagement with God's written words.

On one hand, if the sermon is the primary way people engage the Bible during a given week, the preacher can—even if unintentionally—become the mediator between God and man. If we rely too much on a teacher's study and explanation, we hinder people's everyday engagement of God's perfect Word, modeling for them instead that our imperfect words are a more nourishing aspect of their spiritual diet. (And we perpetuate this if small group discussion guides point to what teachers say on Sundays over what the Bible says every day.)

On the other hand, many churches today stand in contrast to, say, the apostle Paul's example to the church at Ephesus. Before leaving Ephesus to continue God's mission in another place, he claimed, "I did not shrink from declaring to you the whole counsel of God" (Acts 20:27). Instead of helping God's people understand *all* of Scripture, many churches instead focus on a few parts. And I have found this to be true across church traditions.

It would be nearly impossible to thoroughly teach through every biblical book and theme in a lifetime of Sundays. Plus, churches often avoid biblical books that are hard to teach—and there are many!

I was baptized Catholic as a baby, and my formative years were spent in a mainline Protestant tradition. Teaching in many Roman Catholic and mainline denominations is based on a *lectionary*. These annual or multiyear cycles of Scripture passages vary by denomination. But after surveying the current Roman Catholic lectionary, data scientist and practicing Catholic Stefan Avey concludes, "a Catholic who attends Mass on Sundays and Feasts (but not weekdays) would hear ~ **4%** of the Old Testament (excluding Psalms) and ~ **41%** of the New Testament" in a given year (emphasis in original).[3]

Avey's response? "Wow—this was a shock to me! I bet if you ask around you'll hear that many Catholics think the lectionary includes the whole Bible. To be fair, these numbers do get a bit higher if you include the complete lectionary (with weekdays). The total coverage of the Old Testament is ~**14%** (again excluding Psalms) and for the New Testament it is ~**72%**."[4] But only one percent of Catholics feel called to daily mass.[5]

Alternatively, in evangelical and nondenominational churches —like those I've attended and served most of my adult life— teaching is often based on a "sermon series," in which a teacher or team divides up a biblical book or theme, or merely a topic they want to teach, then does a deep dive into it over a number of weeks, months, or even years. It would be nearly impossible to thoroughly teach through every biblical book and theme in a lifetime of Sundays. I can assure you that in twenty years, I've not taught even half the Bible. Also, in most churches, these series trend heavily toward the New Testament and even repeat some books over the years, rather than rotating through all sixty-six books of the Bible. Plus, they often avoid the books that are hard to teach—and *oh man,* there are many!

So, two themes exist between our personal engagement with Scripture and the way churches commonly form God's people to engage God's words: our Bible reading is limited in general, and it's limited with regard to the portions and likely genres within the Bible we read. This first symptom of missing the gospel in the Bible might be one of "quantity": we don't read the Bible much.

DON'T READ THE BIBLE IN THESE "LITTLE BITS"

But there's a "quality" issue at play too. Even if we do read the Bible, many of us don't know how to read it well. In *The Drama of Scripture*, Craig Bartholomew and Mike Goheen summarize this second symptom, and the danger thereof:

> Many of us have read the Bible as if it were merely a mosaic of little bits—theological bits, moral bits, historical-critical bits, sermon bits, devotional bits. But when we read the Bible in such a fragmented way, we ignore its divine author's intention to shape our lives through its story. All human communities live out of some story that provides a context for understanding the meaning of history and gives shape and direction to their lives. If we allow the Bible to become fragmented, it is in danger of being absorbed into whatever *other* story is shaping our culture, and it will thus cease to shape our lives as it should. Idolatry has twisted the dominant cultural story of the secular Western world. If as believers we allow this story (rather than the Bible) to become the foundation of our thoughts and actions, then our lives will manifest not the truths of Scripture but the lies of an idolatrous culture. Hence, the unity of Scripture is no minor matter: a fragmented Bible may actually produce theologically orthodox, morally upright, warmly pious idol worshipers![6]

None of these "bits" are the right key to unlock the door to the depth of God's message; none is the right lens for reading the Bible. And the authors' ominous charge is that "a fragmented Bible may actually produce theologically orthodox, morally upright, warmly pious idol worshipers." Let's see what they mean.

Figuring God Out: "Theological Bits"

Theology is the study of God. And the Bible *is* theological: God often reveals Himself through His written words. The Bible *does* tell us about God; through it we can grow in our knowledge of God, His character and attributes, His work and ways. But while the Bible is theological, it is not primarily a *theology* book. Studies of anything are removed from the thing being studied, while the Bible means to draw us closer to God. Studies are also head-focused, but while the Bible informs our heads, it also ignites our hearts and inspires our hands. As English New Testament scholar N. T. Wright puts it,

> The long story of God's plan to put things right, starting with Abraham, climaxing in Jesus and the Spirit, and looking ahead to the new heavens and new earth, isn't the story of guilty humans being forgiven so they could go to heaven, but of idolatrous (and yes, therefore guilty) humans being rescued in order to be worshippers and workers in God's restoration movement, God's kingdom-project.[7]

Finally, studies focus on knowing *about* something, while through the Bible God invites us to move beyond merely knowing *about* Him, to truly, deeply knowing Him.

Some Christians read the Bible hoping to know more about God, or we read the Bible to figure God out. We're thus frustrated when God's unfathomable depths are not fully explained, when

His mysteries remain mysterious, when stories seem illogical, and even when Jesus' words to one audience seem to contradict His words to another audience. The Bible teaches us about God, but also does so much more.

Changing Our Behavior: "Moral Bits"

Every culture loves morality tales. From Aesop's fables to Mother Goose to Walt Disney, we look for lessons at a story's end. And we like that Jesus spoke in parables. But some Christians read the Bible in a way that reduces it to a tutorial. It's much more than that.

Morality tales most often lead to pithy lessons, which are about some behavior change. "The Boy Who Cried Wolf," for example, teaches us to stop lying. That echoes a biblical value, but the Bible's texts about truth-telling are about a heart change more than behavioral change; they're about increasingly reflecting God, who *is* truth, by the power of His Spirit. "The Tortoise and the Hare" tells us to never give up and to not be lazy, *Finding Nemo* reminds us to "just keep swimming," and so forth. Morality tales tell us if we just do or stop doing something, life is better. That's not always true of life in Christ: indeed, nearly every New Testament book says that in doing good for Jesus, we'll suffer. That's not a fun morality tale!

And as we'll see in the next chapter, we often can't make the change we see in the Bible's verses, commands, or stories. We're left feeling guilty and discouraged, and we either give up or "fake it." Neither of these trails lead to happy endings; neither path is God's heart for His people.

Disregarding the Past: "Historical Bits"

If the Bible is merely history, we get to pick and choose which pieces apply to our lives. Biblical events *are* historical of course: they happened in very real cultures, to very real people, by the power of a very real God. Technology, dating, and archaeology increasingly corroborate the events of the Bible, putting them squarely in the course of human history. And as we'll see in chapter 3, we need to recover the original culture in which various events happened, since original context helps us more rightly understand God's message.

But the Bible is more than a history book. History is human-focused, and thus imperfect; it is fallible and changes over time. The Bible is God-focused and perfect; its original form was inspired by God and, while contextualization is necessary, its principles are unchanging. If the Bible is merely a historical record, we can choose parts we don't like, attribute them to long-outdated ethics of an ancient society, and live as if the authority behind the command no longer exists. But Jesus' followers believe that God, who inspired the Bible and surpasses human history, is alive, and that His word is as poignant and applicable today as when each biblical book was penned.

Feeling Good: "Devotional Bits"

A "devotion" in many Christian circles is a proactive time to focus, often on a short but powerful resource that gives inspiration for anything from a single moment to a season or lifetime. Numerous books and websites exist under the category of "devotional." These can be good, and the Bible *does* contain powerful verses and inspirational stories, but the Bible is not just a "devotion."

A devotional reading of the Bible commonly focuses on building oneself up; we look to the Bible for inspiration, often some form of "you're great; you can do it." On one hand, this puts all the effort on the reader to do whatever "it" is, which is the opposite of the biblical message.

My friend and Dallas pastor Kendrick Banks jokes that this way of reading the Bible is "perfect for perpetuating our problematic individualistic church culture. This form of misapplying verses is only as effective as pinning any positivity quote to the wall or seeking a fortune cookie for moral encouragement." On the other hand, "you can do it" might simply be a false sentiment. Some days are hard. We might fail at something we're trying to do. Reading the Bible to make ourselves feel good about ourselves can feel cathartic for a moment, but it's not what God intended for His people or His words. It might even cause us to doubt God if we realize we *can't* do what we interpret the Bible to say we *can* do. So, while the Bible *does* speak to our hearts and hands, its message is not primarily an emotional boost to get us over some proverbial hump.

A Rule Book or a Quick Fix

While the previous categories expand on Bartholomew and Goheen's quote, the most common definition I've heard of the Bible is "a list of rules." Of course, the Bible does include God's commands. Some of us try to follow out of sheer obedience; sometimes our obedience is earnest and sometimes it's out of guilt or fear of God's punishment; other times it's rote and dry. Sometimes we understand the words we read, though often they seem distant or confusing. Many simply seem impossible. And often, as with New Year's resolutions, our resolve only lasts so long. God did not give us the Bible merely as a rule book!

Finally, some read the Bible seeking a guaranteed fix to something that's off in our lives. God does offer a solution, but we love claiming the Bible's promises as our own, even if they're out of context and apply zero percent to our situation. We might print verses out, post them on our bathroom mirror or steering wheel, and commit them to memory. Sometimes, the passages come to mind and help us; other times, they feel condemning. We may think God let us down when He doesn't keep the out-of-context promise we claimed as our own.

> There are good reasons for finding certain Scriptures at certain times. But if that's all we know to do, we miss the unity of the whole Bible. Or, we see the words on the page but miss the truly good news they carry.

HOW DO YOU READ THE BIBLE?

There are other wrong lenses to read the Bible through. Pastor and author Dane Ortlund notes several; for instance, the "gold mine approach." This is when we occasionally come upon a "nugget of inspiration." He also describes the "magic eight-ball approach," when we read the Bible as a road map for major decisions.[8] Some people go to the Bible seeking contradictions, trying to disprove it, or finding reasons not to obey. Others tackle it like a textbook, to be dissected and analyzed. And so forth. These miss the point as well.

But while each common lens above is unique and nuanced, an underlying thread connects all of them: these approaches to the Bible focus on the *words* of the text but miss the true *Word*. Jesus is the very *Word* of God (John 1:1). He's the embodiment of each truth in the Bible, the perfection that each imperfect hero of every Bible story points to, and the ultimate fulfillment of every command and promise. His gospel is the key to reading the Bible rightly. That's the diagnosis we'll find in the next chapter, based on a shocking lack of quality and quantity in our Bible reading.

Charlotte still sometimes only rereads the parts of Harry Potter she likes, and I'm fine with that. Of course, there are good reasons for finding certain Scriptures at certain times, and it's helpful for churches, groups, households, and individuals to dive deeply into specific texts; these can help us know and dwell with God in the Bible's intricately described commands and stories. But if that's all we know to do, we miss the unity of the whole Bible. Or, we see the words on the page but miss the truly good news they carry.

In other words, we read the Bible but miss the gospel.

The question remains regarding this chapter's symptoms: Which are true of you? How do you read the Bible? What lens, or lenses, do you see God's Word through? Perhaps you have only ever read the Bible through one of those "little bits" lenses, or a combination. Perhaps you have never thought there might be a different approach to God's Word. But there is, and that is what we will explore in the next chapter.

To Think About and Discuss

1. What has been your view of the Bible and its importance? How was that view formed?

2. How often do you read your Bible, and what is your primary motive for reading it?

3. Which "little bits" category best describes your posture when you read the Bible: Do you hope to figure God out, change your behavior, learn historic facts, feel better about yourself, or learn rules to follow? Or something else entirely?

4. What do you think might be the danger of the "little bits" categories in this chapter? How do you think they miss God's intention?

5. In what ways do you think the gospel—the good news of Jesus' life, death, resurrection, and reign—should shape our reading of the whole Bible?

6. In what ways do you think you need to trust the gospel and rest in God's grace toward you, even as you start this journey and perhaps change how you read the Bible?

Have this mind among yourselves,
which is yours in Christ Jesus, who, though he was
in the form of God, did not count equality with
God a thing to be grasped, but emptied himself,
by taking the form of a servant, being born in the
likeness of men. And being found in human form,
he humbled himself by becoming obedient to
the point of death, even death on a cross.
Therefore God has highly exalted him and bestowed
on him the name that is above every name.

PHILIPPIANS 2:5–9

CHAPTER 2

DIAGNOSIS: MISSING THE GOSPEL

"THERE IS AN UN-CHRISTIAN WAY TO READ OUR BIBLES."

When I use this phrase in training church leaders on gospel-centered life and ministry, the response is often visual discomfort. But that's nothing compared to the sentence I usually follow up with: "In fact, there are ways to read the New Testament in a way that Muslims and Jews could wholly affirm and agree with. And there are ways to teach the Bible in our churches in the same way it could be taught in a mosque or synagogue."

To be clear, I fully support discussing the Bible among friends with different beliefs; I have the honor of doing so at times. But if we read or teach the Bible without every passage overtly pointing us to Jesus, we are not reading the Bible in a "Christian" way. Let me use a well-known passage throughout this chapter as an illustration to demonstrate the common way we miss the gospel when we read the Bible. Then we'll find the long-awaited remedy, and three steps to establish the right lens through which we find the heart of God's message.

The second chapter of apostle Paul's letter to the Philippians contains some of the best-known verses in the New Testament:

> So if there is any encouragement in Christ, any comfort from love, any participation in the Spirit, any affection and sympathy, complete my joy by being of the same mind, having the same love, being in full accord and of one mind. Do nothing from selfish ambition or conceit, but in humility count others more significant than yourselves. Let each of you look not only to his own interests, but also to the interests of others. Have this mind among yourselves, which is yours in Christ Jesus, who, though he was in the form of God, did not count equality with God a thing to be grasped, but emptied himself, by taking the form of a servant, being born in the likeness of men. And being found in human form, he humbled himself by becoming obedient to the point of death, even death on a cross. Therefore God has highly exalted him and bestowed on him the name that is above every name, so that at the name of Jesus every knee should bow, in heaven and on earth and under the earth, and every tongue confess that Jesus Christ is Lord, to the glory of God the Father. (vv. 1–11)

PHILIPPIANS 2 THROUGH THE WRONG LENSES

This is a familiar passage, and rightly so. It involves a poem, a Jesus-praising hymn that was repeated in the early church. So even if the first symptom in chapter 1 is true of us—lack of quantity in our Bible reading—these might be verses we have come across, have been taught, or have tried to memorize and follow. But to address the previous chapter's second symptom—lack of quality in our Bible reading—what happens if we read these verses through a wrong lens? Let's try reading this passage through the "little bits."

Philippians 2 as Theology

This passage contains rich theology: we see that Jesus left His rightful throne, and went through a three-step process of humbling Himself:

He took the form of a human servant;
He fully obeyed, to the point of death;
He endured crucifixion, the highest form of humiliation.

Then we see Jesus exalted, being returned by God the Father to His rightful throne. His rule is not just for now, but will last forever as everything on earth will one day declare Him Lord. We see in these some inter-trinitarian dynamics, and we discover that through Jesus' humility and exaltation, (a) God the Father was glorified, and (b) we are motivated to be unified and humble. This is one common way to read this text. We are left knowing more about our triune God, understanding how God's actions worked, and the process Jesus went through. We see one way that God is glorified, and we are told that Jesus' humility should motivate our own. We close our Bibles, having figured out a little more about God and understanding the logic of the text.

Philippians 2 as a Morality Tale

As mentioned above, at face value, Philippians 2 could fit the "morality tale" genre nicely: look at the example, learn from it, and do likewise. In this passage, Paul tells a story about Jesus, who did something good and received a reward for doing that good thing. Jesus was willing to be humbled, serve God, and die for people . . . and God exalted Him. So, as some people have been taught over time, the moral of the story seems to be that if we just humble ourselves like Jesus did, God will exalt us too. Of course, we won't be as exalted as Jesus, but then we don't humble ourselves to the point He humbled Himself either. This is another common way to read the text. If we're honest, we know we're not humble by nature, so we might leave this text committing to "be like Jesus"; to be humbler— perhaps so that God will reward us for doing the right thing.

Philippians 2 as History

Historians might tell you that at the time Paul wrote this, Philippi was a Roman colony, on the main east-west road across the Roman empire in northern Greece. We might learn that the rally cry across the empire in the AD 50s was the "good news" of Caesar Augustus's rule. Philippians, the historians might say, shows us the countercultural cry of God's people. That is, Jesus' rule was better than Caesar's, and thus the "good news" of Jesus surpassed Caesar.

We might see that in this context, Philippians 2 teaches a power dynamic that opposes the world, and that Jesus' humility was a model for the new and fragile church in the midst of a mighty Roman world. I personally love culture and history, and frankly, believe that Jesus' followers would better understand the Bible if we knew the nuances of the first-century world. But if Philippians 2 is mere history, then the message is limited to those in northern Greece in the AD 50s. Readers in the United States, for example, don't have context for a monarch, and even modern kings and queens are different than first-century emperors. If the Bible is history, we can read it as such: its message is disconnected from our lives, and while we might pick up a lesson here and there, it's largely just information about a time gone by.

Philippians 2 as Devotion

A devotional reading of Philippians 2 would focus on the depth of Jesus' love for us—"He was willing to give up heaven and die . . . for you!" God was pleased with Jesus, and Jesus glorified God, and one day Jesus will be Lord of everything.

Based on the amazing love of God, the focus of a devotional reading of this text would then be on the outcome of the unity that Jesus' humility inspires: we feel affection for God and others, sympathy and love for people, and we find encouragement in Christ and comfort from His love, no matter what today holds. Like Paul asked the Philippians to complete His joy, so also do we know that God will complete our joy today, because He loves us that much.

We might end our reading with a satisfied smile, relishing in God's goodness toward us, feeling bolstered by His love, and ready to take on anything the day has in store. We know that whatever comes our way, we'll face it with the Spirit's participation, and Jesus encouraging and comforting us.

Philippians 2 as Rules

If we think of the Bible primarily as a rulebook, we'll find this passage chock-full of new laws to obey:

1. "Be of the same mind, have the same love, and be in full accord and of one mind with others" (v. 2).
2. "Do nothing from selfish ambition or conceit" (v. 3).
3. "Count others more significant than yourselves" (v. 3).
4. "Look not to your own interest, but also to the interests of others" (v. 4).
5. Have the mind of Christ. This is a paraphrase of v. 5; through an action-oriented lens, "have" likely means "go find it" or "attain it."

There's a lot to *do* in these verses. We read them, skip over the part about Jesus, and declare ourselves up for the challenge. Perhaps we do so thinking we can earn more of God's love if we can accomplish the mission we think He's sending us off to with these marching orders.

Philippians 2 as a Quick Fix

Church leaders might be the worst at using the Bible as a quick fix. Maybe a husband is talking to his pastor about an argument with his wife when the pastor, nodding empathetically, breaks in. "You know, sounds like you were being kind of prideful. It makes me think of Philippians 2, where we see the extent of Jesus' humility. You might go home and read that and think about whether or not you loved your wife the way that Jesus loves you." (You can almost see the pastor's hand on the husband's shoulder, gently escorting him out of the office.) The quick fix in this case uses Philippians 2 like the legendary doctor who says, "Take two aspirins and call me in the morning." We think that just reading some verses once will make everything better.

PRETENDING AND PERFORMING

The summaries of the wrong lenses above are perhaps generalized and a bit overstated. But each is also an actual way that I've heard this particular passage summarized, used, or taught over the years. There are positive elements in seeing the passage through many of those lenses, but all of them fall short of finding God's heart—the Bible's true message—in this passage.

A simple summary of the passage could be this command: "Be unified and humble, because Jesus humbled Himself even more." That is a fair summary; it's what the words on the page of this specific portion of the Bible say. Paul overtly points to Jesus as our example for following this command, which Paul himself doesn't always do. At face value, then, this text seems Christ-centered and applicable: "As a follower of Jesus, do what Jesus did." If that seems too simplistic, it's simply a summary of an inductive method of Bible study in which you cover:

Observation: What does the passage say?

Interpretation: What does it mean?

Application: What does it mean to me?

Anyone who has ever tried to "apply" this verse by their own power knows the folly of that endeavor. Making ourselves humble or "considering others more highly than ourselves" isn't something we can conjure up. But if we read the passage through one of these poor lenses, we know that we're supposed to apply the verse to our lives. So we try.

What happens when we find ourselves unable to meet God's command for humility—or any other command in the Bible, for that matter? Authors Bob Thune and Will Walker say we turn one of two ways: pretending or performing. "Pretending minimizes sin by making ourselves out to be something we are not. Performing minimizes God's holiness by reducing his standard to something we can meet."[1] In other words, we pretend. We put on an outward humility that doesn't reflect our true hearts or minds. Or we perform. We convince ourselves that we're "humble enough," bringing God's perfect standard down to a version we can attain. Both ways, we're focusing on what we're able to do more than what God is able to do and has done in the gospel. Thune and Walker say we "shrink the cross," because both ways miss the gospel.[2]

On the surface, this is the command: "Be like Jesus." This is also why our monotheistic cousins could read and teach this passage the same way. Many Jews and Muslims believe Jesus was a good teacher whose example should be followed. As they strive to live well, do right, and establish increasing favor with their God, a version of "look at Jesus and do what He did" could be pursued and taught in either of these religious traditions. If that's true, then this way of understanding these verses is still "un-Christian."

This is what I'm getting at. There is a way to read the Bible (the written words) but miss the gospel, which is the incarnate Word made flesh. When we do this, we negate the impact that Jesus actually has on every text, story, and command—and thus on every aspect of our lives. We shrink the cross.

FINDING THE GOSPEL

There's the answer! It's using the right lens, which is the key to reading the Bible as God intended.

Then what *is* a "Christian" way to read or teach Philippians 2 and any other passage? My middle child, Maggie, and I are walking through *The New City Catechism* as I write this:

the kids' version is a yearlong series of weekly questions and answers, describing foundational aspects of faith. Maggie calls it her "Little Bible" (which it isn't, but she's cute so I let it slide), and three weeks of questions and answers help us understand a "truly Christian" way to read the Bible—that is, the key to reading the Bible without missing the gospel. Let's look at two examples:

"What does the law of God require? That we love God with all our heart, soul, mind, and strength; and love our neighbor as ourselves."

"Can anyone keep the law of God perfectly? Since the fall, no mere human has been able to keep the law of God perfectly."[3]

These two questions and answers summarize what many people feel when they read the Bible's commands: God tells us in the Bible that He expects perfection, but we can't ever be perfect! And again, this gospel-less interpretation leads us to a pattern of trying and failing, eventually pretending or performing, and finally giving up, feeling defeated, or putting on an outward act. But there's a blessed third question that brings everything into focus:

"Since no one can keep the law, what is its purpose? That we may know the holy nature and will of God, and the sinful nature and disobedience of our hearts; *and thus our need of a Savior*" (emphasis added)."[4]

There's the answer! It's using the right lens, which is the key to reading the Bible as God intended. In every verse, command, and story of the Bible, God shows us His nature (perfect holiness), and by contrast, shows us our nature (imperfect and sinful). But the point of Philippians 2 and every other command in the Bible is not to make us work more, try harder, or turn toward what we can do. Rather, it's to help us realize how inadequate we are, and turn to Jesus, who *does* have the power to do in and through us, by the power of His Spirit, all we cannot do on our own. Jesus is thus not only the truest model of perfect humility, but His Spirit is the truest source of any personal humility we can hope for. God is both our example and our power, if we want to live the fruitful life seen in these verses.

THE "CHRISTIAN WAY" TO READ PHILIPPIANS 2

The "Christian way" to read Philippians 2 and every other part of the Bible is to do so in a way that starts and ends with God rather than with people. The "Christian way" to read every passage is one that draws us into dependence on God rather than on ourselves or anything else but Him, reading in a way that we see the true change that Jesus makes in our daily lives.

To be clear, this passage *is* meant to be an example for us to follow, just as we must seek obedience to *every* biblical command. But rather than feeling defeated by our inability, the right lens of the gospel actually leads us to great freedom. By admitting our need for a Savior, we declare that the core tenet of our faith is indeed true, not just one time at the start of our walk with God, but true every day. Any hope we have for obedience isn't from our own power: "If we live by the Spirit, let us also keep in step with the Spirit" (Gal. 5:25). We know:

God is strong when we are weak.

His grace is sufficient for us.

He can do far more than we can ask or think.

What is impossible with man is possible with God.

These statements are from commonly taught verses, and perhaps feel cliché after a time.[5] But only when we connect these truths to every passage of Scripture, like Philippians 2—which are sealed in

Jesus' life, death, resurrection, and reign—do we find the core truth of this book. That is how we apply gospel truths to our reading of the Bible. In this, we read the Bible in a truly "Christian way."

What does this look like in practice in this chapter's Philippians 2 example?

Jesus' *life* is our example of humility. He perfectly reflected His Father's will through His actions, spoke only God's words, and was perfectly obedient in all things.

Jesus' *death* paid the price for our sin and imperfection, including our lack of humility, so even when we don't meet God's standard or follow Jesus' example, we get to rest in God's forgiveness and grace; we are still pure because of Jesus' humble death.

In His *resurrection,* Jesus ushered in a new life and sent us His Spirit to live in us and empower us to increasingly—albeit sometimes slowly—become like Jesus. This happens as God grows our humility, turns us away from the self-reliance that leads us to perform and pretend, and teaches us to rely on Him more and more, abiding in Him, and trusting Him to produce fruit.

And Jesus' *reign* as king, which is already true for this life as well as the next, gives us a better motive for humility: we live for a better King and kingdom than any on earth. His reign gives us a better promise: one day all brokenness (including pride) will be gone, and we will be perfectly humble, fulfilling the commands of Philippians 2 as fully restored people, living fully under Jesus' kingship for all eternity.

THE "CHRISTIAN WAY" TO READ OUR BIBLES

There are other ways the gospel lens shapes our reading of Philippians 2. In fact, the truths of Jesus' life, death, resurrection, and reign are innumerable. But reading those verses through the lens of the gospel—trusting not only Jesus' example, but also depending on His Spirit to produce any obedience in us as we recall such things as His forgiveness, grace, empowerment, motive, and power —is what creates a uniquely "Christian" reading of these verses; it's what sets our faith apart from any other. As we've seen, the lenses we typically have and have at times been taught can lead us to miss the gospel as we read the Bible. The next chapter helps us fix that problem. We'll discover the remedy.

To Think About and Discuss

1. What things were new, different, helpful, or hard for you as you read this chapter?

2. In chapter 1's discussion, which "little bits" category/ categories did you say best describe your posture when you read the Bible?

3. After reading chapter 2, what would you see as the danger of reading the Bible through "little bits" lenses?

4. When have you found yourself pretending or performing— either putting on an outward show you know doesn't match your heart or trying so hard (and at times failing) to meet the seemingly impossible standards we read in the Bible? How do those realities hinder your relationship with God and others?

5. How will it look for you to stop working more, trying harder, and turning toward what you can do as you read the Bible, and instead realize your inadequacy and turn to Jesus, who, by His Spirit, can do in and through us all we cannot do on our own?

6. In what ways do you think you'll need to trust the gospel and rest in God's grace toward you, even as you pursue this view of reading the Bible in your everyday life?

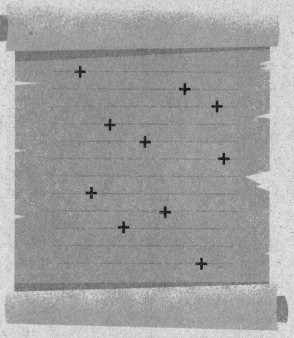

And beginning with Moses and all the Prophets, he interpreted to them in all the Scriptures the things concerning himself. . . .

And their eyes were opened, and they recognized him. And he vanished from their sight. They said to each other, "Did not our hearts burn within us while he talked to us on the road, while he opened to us the Scriptures?"

LUKE 24:27, 31–32

CHAPTER 3

REMEDY:
THE RIGHT LENS
FOR OUR
EVERYDAY LIVES

BC AND AD MEAN MORE FOR US THAN WE KNOW

For much of modern history, global events, dates, and even time itself was divided into two categories: BC, "Before Christ," and AD, *anno domini,* Latin for "the year of our Lord."

In the first decades after Jesus ascended, His life, death, resurrection, and reign made such an obvious difference in the lives of His followers that it confused and confounded everyone around them as the Christian message expanded across the Roman Empire. By the sixth century, Jesus' life, death, resurrection, and reign were recognized to be such a clear turning point that history's calculation of time was centered around it.

So, a monk of that time named Dionysius Exiguus placed history into two distinct eras, centering on the approximate date of Jesus' birth. For the past 1,500 years, this generally accepted division of time bases all of history around Jesus: the years before His birth get higher and higher the further back they go from His life, and the years after similarly get higher as more years pass from His birth. In a growing pluralist global culture, these monikers are being increasingly replaced with CE, "common era," and BCE, "before common era," which stick to the same years (AD 525 is 525 CE and so forth). But whatever letters we use, Dionysius created this system to define one unifying, global standard to mark time.

But the singular life he chose to base it on was indeed the dividing point in history.

Here's an example of this. The book of Hebrews clearly says that because of Jesus' death, Israel's daily sacrifices, which had been a cornerstone of worship for millennia, were no longer necessary. Jesus, the full and final sacrifice, fulfilled that aspect of worship and redefined the life of God's people. AD life, if you will, would look different than it had BC. What made the difference? The gospel, the defining point of all history.

Similarly, we read in the New Testament that things that had once been separated were brought together, based on the shared blood of Christ that gave Jews and Gentiles, slaves and free, male and female a greater identity and unity. The people of God AD would look different than the people of God BC. What caused the change? The gospel.

There are many verses and themes in the Bible where we clearly see Jesus' life, death, resurrection, and reign changing everything. But what if there are other verses and themes that we still misread? What if we've missed the massive difference Jesus makes to understanding sin and asking for God's forgiveness, or to our places and forms of worship, or to our definition of God's blessing, or even the gospel itself?

In day-to-day ways, I wonder if faithful followers of Jesus like you and me still largely assume BC ways of living out our faith and relating to God and others, even in this AD era. We can find dozens of areas of life and faith in which I believe we've missed the gospel, to the detriment of our understanding of God and to our faith, lives, and relationships.

After considering the symptoms in chapter 1 and discovering the diagnosis for reading the Bible but missing the gospel in chapter 2, this chapter offers a remedy. We finally receive the prescription for a new lens, through which we can see the Bible rightly.

ᴗᴗ SEEING CLEARLY

Symptoms: Lack of quantity: we don't read the Bible much; and our quality is lacking when we view Scripture in "little bits."

Diagnosis: We miss this: that the gospel of Jesus is the key to reading the Bible correctly.

Remedy: Prayerfully take three steps to find the right lens every time you read the Bible (they're described in this chapter).

But more than merely helping us read the Bible better, this new lens truly changes our lives. We've discussed how Jesus' life, death, and resurrection is the key to grasping God's message more clearly, but now we'll look at how that message has more impact than perhaps we previously realized—on our walk with God, our relationships with others, and our everyday existence. This new— or rather, ancient—lens will likely challenge ways we've thought of life and faith and will help us worship and appreciate God more fully as we see the depth and breadth of His good news for our lives.

A THREEFOLD REMEDY THAT CHANGES EVERYTHING

To get more specific, learning to read the Bible through the lens of the gospel can be summarized as a threefold process. Adjusting to this new lens won't happen overnight, and we'll spend the rest of the book learning to see the Bible through this new lens and living accordingly. But getting the Bible right in everyday life starts with three steps:

- Reading the Bible as God's story
- Knowing where we are in the story
- Learning to see Jesus as the hero and Redeemer

Together, these help us relearn to read the Bible through the right lens of the gospel. Let's take a look at each.

Reading the Bible as God's Story

What is the dominant story of your life? Everyone has a person, event, identity, or theme that shapes us. A friend of mine is an NFL MVP: that award still shapes his life nearly two decades later. Another friend feels defined primarily by her upbringing as an adopted child of one ethnicity in a family from another ethnicity. Our dreams and our culture shape our dominant story, and so forth. Whatever shapes your story also shapes the way you read the Bible.

In chapter 1, we warned against reading the Bible as "little bits" of theology, morality tales, history, devotion, rules, or quick fixes. Remember, "if we allow the Bible to become fragmented, it is in danger of being absorbed into whatever *other* story is shaping our culture, and it will thus cease to shape our lives as it should."[1]

To rightly see the Bible as one, cohesive story, we must see the

Bible as the story of God. And we must accept it as the dominant story, written by the one Author who alone has the authority to shape all of life. God tells His one unified story in the Bible in multiple broad acts, each involving different characters, verses, commands, and stories. These can be summarized in six acts as follows:

ACT 1, CREATION (Gen. 1–2): God created everything good, right, and beautiful. He lovingly made people to cultivate His creation alongside Him, at peace with Him, one another, and all creation.

ACT 2, REBELLION (Gen. 3–11): The first people rebelled against God's reign. They decided God was holding back good things from them and wanted to decide for themselves what was right and wrong. The result was that human sin entered God's good creation and all creation came under a curse. Everything was affected by this rebellion.

ACT 3, PROMISE (Gen. 12–Malachi): God did not leave His rebellious people without hope. He decided to rescue His creation by calling one man named Abram (later renamed Abraham) and making him into a great nation. Through this nation, Israel, God was going to bless all the other nations. But just like the first people, they rebelled too, over and over throughout the Old Testament.

ACT 4, REDEMPTION (Gospels): When all seemed lost, God was faithful to His promise. Jesus, God's own Son, came to be the promised deliverer and perfectly obeyed the Father. The kingdom had come near. But the people rebelled against Jesus and put Him to death on a cross. When Jesus was put to death, He took on the curse of creation and bore the burden of people's sin. He then accomplished victory over all evil through His resurrection.

Restoration had begun, new creation was here, and Jesus was the true and risen King.

ACT 5, CHURCH (Acts–Jude): The resurrected Jesus sent His Spirit to empower His followers to demonstrate and declare the good news that God was restoring the world and that Jesus is King! He alone can save and bring the peace we all so desperately desire. People are now invited to give their allegiance to Jesus and live according to His story. Forgiveness, hope, and salvation are possible because of Jesus. This is the church, the act of the story we find ourselves in today.

ACT 6, RESTORATION (Revelation): One day King Jesus will return to finally and fully make the world the way it is supposed to be. He will bring justice, healing, and wholeness. There will be no more tears, pain, sickness, brokenness, or death. Those who have declared allegiance to Jesus as King and by faith depended on Him for salvation will forever enjoy His presence; but those who chose to rely on themselves and false saviors will be forever separated from His good reign. We pray for the day of His return to come quickly![2]

That's the Bible's one story. And there are many characters in that story—good and evil ones; human and spiritual beings. But from start to finish, there's one main character: God.

Within each of these acts, we see that one, history-long gospel story is also told over and over again in the Bible, in many smaller stories. Time and time again, we see God as powerful and good, mighty and caring, able and patient. For example, here is the pattern of the Old Testament's narratives: Israelites are enslaved in Egypt; God saves them through Moses. God's people rebel again and again; God calls them back, at various points through priests, judges, kings, and prophets. The whole Old Testament tells and retells the story of creation, rebellion, promise, redemption, and at least partial restoration. The Old Testament stories are microcosms of humanity's greatest rebellion, our need for deeper redemption, and God's promised, coming restoration. The Old Testament foreshadows Jesus' life, death, resurrection, and reign.

THE BIBLE: MANY STORIES TELLING ONE STORY

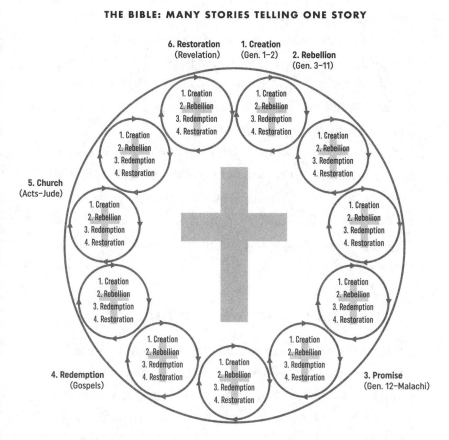

In the New Testament, the pattern repeats in the lives of several figures and those they interact with. For example, Jesus gave Peter a calling, but in a key moment he denied Jesus. Jesus forgave him, giving him a new calling and commission, restoring him to become a vital part of God's first-century mission. God created Saul of Tarsus, who was devoted to knowing God. But he became a murderer of Christians. Only through Jesus' overt intervention was Saul saved and became the influential apostle we know today. The book of Acts and the New Testament letters address real scenarios in the lives of real people at real points in history. The letters' authors remind readers of God's goodness, our rebellion, God's redemptive work in the gospel, and how God empowers us to right living by His Spirit under Jesus' reign. Finally, John describes a full and final cosmic rebellion—and also God's victory and the full and final restoration all creation longed for since Genesis 3 brought brokenness into the world.

This summary of the Bible is admittedly general and brief. But it also gives the broad contours to help us rightly read the Bible: if we see the Bible less as history or morality tales, for example, and more the story of God, then we approach the Scriptures primarily looking for ways God is telling His own story. That's the first step toward a remedy.

KNOWING WHERE WE ARE IN THE STORY

Seeing the Bible as God's story helps us remember where we fit into it. Understanding the realities of a given context and culture about whom or to whom a biblical book or letter was written matters as we try to interpret the words of that book and its implications for our lives today. If God gave an "Act 3" promise to His covenant nation Israel in the Old Testament, we cannot claim that it automatically applies to any nation, that exists in this age—that is, the age between His ascension and His return.

Similarly, at specific times in history, God's presence dwelled in a specific place—first the wilderness tabernacle, then the Jerusalem temple. But at Jesus' last breath on Good Friday, God tore the temple curtain, and gave all people direct access to Himself. Today the "Holy Spirit . . . *dwells within us*" (2 Tim. 1:14). In the gospel, God's very dwelling place changed. And let's make it practical: How often are we welcomed "into the house of the Lord" as a worship service begins? It's a common thing to say, but has it dawned on us that it's imprecise? We're using BC words for an AD truth.

Dozens of misunderstandings like this invade Christian understanding and church teaching: we miss the gospel! In Part Two we'll flesh this out, looking at commonly misunderstood areas of life and faith.

Knowing where scriptural passages fit and knowing where we fit into God's story can clear up much misunderstanding and misinterpretation of the Bible. To better understand how a given verse, command, or story might relate to you, try these four questions, which I first learned from my friend Jeff Vanderstelt.[3]

1. **WHO IS GOD?** What do these verses tell me is true of God's character and being—whether I believe it or not?
2. **WHAT DOES GOD DO?** What do these verses tell me is true of God's activity, work, and promises—especially through the life, death, resurrection, and reign of Jesus— and again, whether I believe it or not?
3. **WHO ARE WE?** What do these verses tell me is true of mankind, and thus myself—positive or negative—and whether I believe it or not?

4. **WHAT DO WE DO?** Based on the other three questions,
what might God be leading us—or me—to do, by the
power of His Spirit, through these verses?

Learning to See Jesus as the Hero and Redeemer

Every Bible story's human hero was imperfect—but each reflects some attributes of Jesus, who alone is perfect. Every command of the Bible similarly reflects a standard that Jesus alone
meets. And as we've said, the whole Bible (and every verse in
it), points to Jesus. In this, Jesus is the hero of the Bible. But, as
my friend and Western Seminary professor Dr. Gerry Breshears
wisely points out, there's a danger with the phrase "seeing Jesus
as the hero": "it leads to Him as our moral example rather than
our Savior, which is just another form of what [this book is] trying to correct."[4] Gerry is right: Jesus' role as we learn to read the
Bible rightly is twofold: Jesus *is* the perfect example the whole
Bible points us to. And Jesus is more: by His Spirit He is the very
source of strength and power for any true and lasting fruit, any
heart change, any reconciliation, and any obedience in aspects of
our own faith, lives, and relationships. Both at the beginning of
our Christian walk and in some area of our lives every single day,
Jesus is our true hero and Redeemer.

To learn to see Jesus as the hero and Redeemer, we need to get
in the habit of asking a fifth question: **HOW DOES THIS PASSAGE
POINT TO JESUS?**

There are many ways that Bible texts point us to Jesus, but here
are some common ones to look for.

Prophecy: multiple Old Testament prophets and parts of several psalms predict various aspects of the coming Messiah, which
are later fulfilled in Jesus.

Fulfillment: the Bible often displays human needs and also shows that Jesus fulfills God's promises. When we find a need or promise, we are driven to understand how Jesus is the fulfillment of either.

Comparison/Contrast: we find examples of godly and ungodly people throughout the Bible. If we dig under the surface of their action or inaction, we can find in each a comparison or contrast with the heart of God, which we know Jesus alone perfectly reflects.

Words and Works: by far the clearest way the Bible points to Jesus is by recording His words and works in the gospel accounts. Here we see Jesus as the hero and redeemer of every scene.

Types and Imitations: before we get into types, let's distinguish between type and allegory. Allegory is a long metaphor. An Old Testament example of an allegory would be when the prophet Nathan called out David's sin through the parable of the rich man swiping a poor man's sheep in 2 Samuel 12. New Testament examples of allegory are found in Jesus' parables (e.g., the sower in Matthew 13 and the lost sheep, lost coin, and prodigal son of Luke 15). A literary example of allegory is C. S. Lewis's Chronicles of Narnia in which Aslan the lion symbolizes Christ.

Typology is a certain kind of symbolism, and specifically "a type in Scripture is a person or thing in the Old Testament that foreshadows a person or thing in the New Testament."[5] So a parable tells a story, while a type foreshadows Jesus. There are many instances of types in Scripture, and once you start to look for these, your reading will be enriched, and you'll find yourself reading through clearer lenses. Here's one: the animal God killed to cover Adam and Eve's shame in Genesis 3:21 was a type: it foreshadowed the greater sacrifice of Jesus to cover our shame and remove our sin. Israel's annual sacrificial Passover lamb, commanded by the Mosaic Law, was similar: Jesus is "the Lamb of God, who takes away the sin of the world!" (John 1:29).

Other types and imitations—foreshadows and echoes of His life, death, resurrection, and reign—exist throughout the Bible. Here are a few:

Adam "was a type of the one who was to come" (Rom. 5:14). He was God's son (Luke 3:38) and the first created man, but Jesus accomplished what Adam did not: He fulfilled God's design for humanity.

Jesus is the true and better Noah's ark; He saves God's people from eternal death (1 Peter 3:20–21).

Moses is another type: through him, God freed His people from slavery in their earthly lives. Through Jesus, God offers to free all people from spiritual slavery for eternity. Jesus is the true and better Moses.

He's the true and better bronze serpent that healed (Num. 21:9).

The story of the tabernacle and its furnishings and how all this foreshadows Jesus is worthy of its own study.

The story of Esther and her cousin Mordecai foreshadow Christ.

Kings and prophets, God's covenants, and the Old Testament Law itself all foreshadow Jesus.

In the New Testament, Jesus' baptism is echoed in the coming of God's Spirit in Acts 2.

We're reminded of His healings, and the forgiveness He offers, as His disciples heal and offer forgiveness throughout Acts.

The apostle Paul muses in Philippians 1 about losing his life for the benefit of others, but Jesus *did* give His life, for a far greater benefit for all people who would trust in Him! Jesus is thus the true and better Paul, true and better baptism, true and better healer, and true and better forgiveness. We could go on.

> See missingthegospel.com for a downloadable exercise, to
> help you increasingly see Jesus as the "true and better" version
> of many things in the Bible, and in our daily lives as well.

THE MAIN CHARACTER AND THE SUPPORTING CAST

Though written over a period of about 1,400 years, in three languages, set in multiple locations, employing several genres, and telling hundreds of stories, the Bible has one main character: God. The pinnacle of God's story is Jesus. My goal in this book is for us to see what we too often miss: that all Scripture points to Jesus. Jesus—not verses, commands, and stories—*is* the power to enliven hearts, revive lives, and restore brokenness. As we read earlier, Jesus Himself warned about not missing the point of Scripture when He corrected the religious teachers. "You search the Scriptures because you think that in *them* you have eternal life," He pointed out. But "it is they that bear witness about *me*" (John 5:39).

Since all Scripture points to Jesus, everyone and everything else finds their place in a supporting role. John the Baptist perfectly captures this posture. "He must increase, but I must decrease" (John 3:30).

👓 SEEING CLEARLY

The Bible says that in the gospel, Jesus is the hero and
redeemer of every story: in His life, death, resurrection,
and reign He does what we cannot. Old Testament stories
foreshadow aspects of Jesus' work and New Testament stories
point back to it. As we read Bible stories, we get to see aspects
of the gospel in each account and celebrate Jesus as the hero
and redeemer of the Bible's story and of our own life.

Yet did you notice that we haven't found ourselves in the Bible? If humans who do appear on the Bible's pages are God's supporting cast, what does that mean for us, who don't turn up in the Bible? We might ask who or what in the story represents what is true of humanity at large. Where does our sin, brokenness, pain, inability exist? Who's running from God? Who's caught in something they need to get out of? Most often, that's where we belong in the Bible's many stories. We're not the hero—we *need* the hero. Our role in the Bible's stories rightly starts by seeing how Jesus is the true and better version of every person in the Bible. We ask how Jesus is a full and final version of whatever other people did (or didn't do) or said (or didn't say). We see how He meets people, does what we cannot, and fulfills promises, redemption, and restoration. That's where we fit in each specific Bible story, which points to the overarching story God's writing throughout history and in our lives.

The Bible doesn't tell us how good we are, or that we can accomplish whatever we put our mind to. God's job is *not* helping those who help themselves. We can't be the heroes of even our own stories, much less God's! This unpopular truth appears throughout Scripture: "For the sake of Christ, then, I am content with weaknesses, insults, hardships, persecutions, and calamities. For when I am weak, then I am strong," and "the Spirit helps us in our weakness," Paul writes (2 Cor. 12:10; Rom. 8:26).

Even Paul's invitation, "Be imitators of me, as I am of Christ" (1 Cor. 11:1) is at least an invitation to deep, abiding dependence on God, for *everything*! This was perhaps the hallmark of Jesus' own life; as Jesus Himself says, "Truly, truly, I say to you, the Son can do nothing of his own accord, but only what he sees the Father doing. For whatever the Father does, that the Son does likewise" (John 5:19).

Our role isn't trying harder, pulling up our bootstraps, and proclaiming, "I can do it!" Rather, our role—in any situation—is admitting, "I can't, but God can! God did!" We aren't heroes; we need a hero. And the good news is that we have one—who lived, died, rose, and reigns. Ours is a better hero, better Savior, and better King than anything else under the sun. Just as Jesus is the hero of the Bible's one big story, and every story in it, Jesus is also the hero in the story of our lives too. And we increasingly understand that as we read the stories of the Bible through the lens of the gospel.

As we turn to Part Two of the book—and every time we open our Bibles going forward—let's pray that God will give us eyes to see the Bible as His story; that He will help us know where we are in the story; and that He will show us Jesus as the hero of the story. These are vital steps in discovering this new lens through which to read the Bible, for which we need His help. This is the remedy.

To Think About and Discuss

1. What things were new, different, helpful, or hard for you as you read this chapter?

2. What would you define as the dominant story in your life? What people, events, or things have primarily shaped your beliefs, decisions, motives, and actions?

3. How important have you considered the distinction of time—before Jesus' resurrection and after it—as you've read the Bible? What are some ways that distinction helps us understand the Bible?

4. How will it look to start asking the four questions every time we read the Bible? What would that change about our understanding of the Bible?

5. How will it look to see the heroes of biblical stories as types or imitations of Jesus, the ultimate hero of the ultimate story, and to increasingly let that shape the story of your own life?

6. In what ways do you think you'll need to trust the gospel and rest in God's grace toward you, even as you increasingly believe and practice this view of the Bible in your everyday life?

PART 2

LEARNING TO SEE CLEARLY

or
Seeing Old Verses
through a New,
Life-Changing Lens

Now I would remind you, brothers,
of the gospel I preached to you,
which you received, in which you stand,
and by which you are being saved,
if you hold fast to the word I preached to you—
unless you believed in vain.

For I delivered to you as of first importance
what I also received:
that Christ died for our sins
in accordance with the Scriptures,
that he was buried; that he was raised on the
third day in accordance with the Scriptures.

1 CORINTHIANS 15:1–4

CHAPTER 4

A GOSPEL-CENTERED GOSPEL

"IF JESUS IS REAL, HE SHOULD MATTER TO ALL OF LIFE"

The phrase may seem like the most obvious thought in the world to you. It now does to me too (at least most days). But to my twenty-year-old self, walking across a university green between classes, it was a revelation. That phrase hit me like a ton of bricks. I knew a lot about Jesus. I was a fairly decent Bible teacher. I had actually been hired as a student pastor two years earlier (and regrettably, two years before I think I actually knew Jesus personally. *Yup*). I knew the basic facts of the gospel message: Jesus died for my sin and had been raised from the dead, and if I believed in Him I could avoid hell and live forever with God in perfect glory.

But like many religious and church-going people, those facts were the extent of the gospel message I'd heard. If I may intentionally over-generalize this in a tongue-in-cheek manner, the gospel message I heard was that *a past event had occurred that greatly benefited my future*. Jesus died for my sins and rose again, and if I believe this I get to go to heaven, hard stop.

Does this sound familiar to a gospel presentation you've heard? Perhaps it is a gospel message you've shared with others.

Praise God, these facts are true! Indeed, Jesus' sacrificial, substitutionary death for the sin of the world; His resurrection, which conquered death for all who believe; and His future restoration of all things including broken people's relationship to our perfect and holy God—these things form part of the foundation of the Christian faith. They are the dividing line we believe separates human from human—or to use Jesus' own language, sheep from goat, or brother from brother. We can praise God for the past and future realities of the good news of Jesus' death and resurrection.

> **Interestingly, the afterlife and eternity—the most consistent theme in gospel presentations today—was not the focus of early Christian gospel.**

But there is more to the story. In this chapter, we look at the first biblical topic we must see through a new lens: we must define the gospel itself the way God defines the gospel! It is common in today's Christian circles to guard against a "works-based gospel" and a "prosperity gospel." These are not biblical definitions of the gospel. But a "past-and-future-only" gospel is also not the whole gospel! The gospel is not *less than* Jesus' past work for our future benefit—but it is *more than* that. The Bible leads us to an understanding of the gospel that is more than Jesus' followers (including you and me!) simply declaring belief in, or confessing faith in, or saying a prayer about, Jesus' finished work one time in our own past. It leads us to a view of the best "good news" that surpasses our mere hope for a mansion in heaven one day in the future.

When we understand this, our eyes are opened, our appreciation and need for Jesus deepens, and we discover how Jesus matters to all of life. His life, death, resurrection, and reign speak to a present reality, not just past and future realities. The gospel has current implications for every moment between when we're saved by grace through faith and when Jesus returns or calls us home. For our past, future, and present, the gospel changes everything.

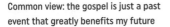

THE GOSPEL FOR ALL OF LIFE

Past	Present	Future

Common view: the gospel is just a past event that greatly benefits my future

Past	Present	Future

Biblical view: the gospel IS a past event that greatly benefits my future . . . and impacts every moment of my present life

AN EXPANSIVE FIRST-CENTURY GOSPEL

"The gospel changes everything" is the primary message of the New Testament. Interestingly, the afterlife and eternity—the most consistent theme in gospel presentations today—was not the focus of the early Christian gospel. N. T. Wright explains, "If that question [of what happens after they died] came up, their answer might be that they would be 'with the Messiah' . . . but they seldom spoke about it at all. They were much more connected with the 'kingdom of God,' which was happening and would ultimately happen completely, 'on earth as it is in heaven.'"[1]

In his gospel, Matthew records Jesus proclaiming this "gospel of the kingdom."[2] Some veins of Christian thinking today see that term as a here-and-now-only message; others see it only as a future and eternal gospel message. This is a false divide, and misses the heart of the gospel, even when defining the gospel! First, "gospel" simply means "good news." We might even say, it's the *best* good news.

Second, looking at Jesus' own life, it would be impossible to say that His "good news" was only focused on a future, afterlife reality. Many theologians see Luke 4 as defining Jesus' life mission: teaching in a Judean synagogue,

> He unrolled the scroll and found the place where it was written,
> "The Spirit of the Lord is upon me,
>> because he has anointed me
>> to proclaim good news to the poor.
> He has sent me to proclaim liberty to the captives
>> and recovering of sight to the blind,
>> to set at liberty those who are oppressed,
> to proclaim the year of the Lord's favor."
> ... "Today this Scripture has been fulfilled in your hearing."
> (Luke 4:17–19, 21)

There is certainly a spiritual sense to what Jesus is saying: in His life, death, and resurrection, He did free spiritual captives, open spiritually blind eyes, and so forth. He ushered in great future hope. But He also opened literal eyes, freed literal oppressed people, and healed so many people He ushered in a present hope!

Third, the gospel of the kingdom was the good news that propelled Jesus' followers to live out their new identity in Christ in the midst of suffering, hatred, persecution, division, danger, and hardship. They saw themselves as citizens of a better kingdom, loyal to a better King than Caesar. This on one hand was treason-ous; only Caesar was Lord in Rome. On the other hand, their faith in Jesus wasn't merely a mental assent to some theology, or an occasional private moment that could be tucked away on some proverbial shelf while Jesus' first-century followers engaged in an otherwise normal life. "In the modern Western world, 'religion' tends to mean God-related individual beliefs and practices that are supposedly separable from culture, politics, and community life. For Paul [and first-century Christians], 'religion' was woven in with all of life."[3]

The "gospel" to Jesus' early followers was one that Jesus saved (past tense), reigns (present tense), and will return (future tense) to restore everything to something better than even the garden of Eden was supposed to be. His followers saw His reign as not just a future reality, but one that began with His ascension—after all, Jesus is seated on His throne now. And they saw their role during their present lives on earth as living in light of that future hope, by the power of Jesus' past resurrection and promised Spirit. They didn't have to decide whether they would proclaim "Jesus saves" *or* love their neighbors and enemies; they didn't choose between pushing folks to be baptized as a declaration of their newfound belief *or* pursuing good works (i.e., living for the good of others, in light of that newfound belief). If Jesus lived, died, rose, and reigns as King forever, then the good news of the kingdom was both a present *and* forever reality: the gospel was both/and, not either/or.

> He changes us in a tangible, every-moment way that impacts every aspect of our present lives.

"I Was This, and Now I'm Something Else"

The good news of Jesus' first coming and its objective change in those whose lives were impacted by that truth fill the first pages of most of the New Testament's letters: "I was *one thing*, and because of Jesus, now I'm *another thing*." "I was dead; I'm now alive." "I was in darkness; now I'm in the light." "I was defined by some lesser story; now I'm defined by the truest story in the whole world." And so forth. In Ephesians 1–3, for example, or Romans 1–11, 1 Peter 1–2, and others, the first portion of many letters tell us what is true of us, whether we believe it or live it or not. Jesus' past work changes our very identity—the core of who we are.

He doesn't only change our identity one time in our own past, that moment or day when we intentionally take a step and declare we believe His work is true. And He doesn't only change it in some ethereal, future way. He changes us in a tangible, every-moment way that impacts every aspect of our present lives.

That same good news, along with the hope of Jesus' second coming, fills the latter pages of each of those same letters (e.g., Eph. 4–6, Rom. 12–16, 1 Peter 3–5), and it was both the motive and power for the renewed and changed walk with God, relationships with others, and daily lifestyle. Because the gospel changed everything.

The Past-Present-Future Gospel

Among numerous examples throughout the New Testament, this message of a past-present-future gospel is found in Ephesians 2:8–10. In the oft-quoted verses 8 and 9, Paul recalls the *past* tense reality of the gospel: "By grace you have been saved through faith. And this is not your own doing; it is the gift of God, not a result of works, so that no one may boast."

Then in the very next verse he emphasizes the *present* tense reality that flows from it: "For we are his workmanship, created in Christ Jesus for good works, which God prepared beforehand, that we should walk in them." In the gospel, God saved us from *past* brokenness. In the gospel, God empowers us for *present* good works.

And in the gospel, verse 7 also gives a glimpse of a glorious *future*: "In the coming ages [God will] show the immeasurable riches of his grace in kindness toward us in Christ Jesus."

Because the gospel changes everything.

This theme is repeated in 2 Corinthians 5:17–20: "If anyone is in Christ, he is a new creation," Paul's thought begins. "The old has passed away; behold, the new has come." What does this look like? Paul explains, starting with God's past tense work: "All this is from God, who through Christ reconciled us to himself and gave us the ministry of reconciliation; that is, in Christ God was reconciling the world to himself, not counting their trespasses against them" (vv. 18–19).

Based on this, the next words shift to the present tense, explaining the gospel implications and even new identity God gives His people, as He is "entrusting to us the message of reconciliation. Therefore, we are ambassadors for Christ, God making his appeal through us" (vv. 19–20). The good news is that Jesus' death and resurrection reconciled us to God, and we are charged to live out our new identity in Christ, by His power and for His glory, in our everyday lives.

Because the gospel changes everything.

Other passages echo similar themes. Perhaps the most overt glimpse of the past, present, and future work of the gospel comes at the end of Paul's first letter to Corinth: "I would remind you, brothers, of the gospel I preached to you," he writes to his friends, "which you *received* [past tense], in which you *stand* [present tense], and by which you *are being saved* [ongoing sense with a view of our future and full salvation], if you hold fast to the word I preached to you" (1 Cor. 15:1–2).

The experience Paul describes is not just true for Jesus' followers in Corinth; all these aspects were the normative message of the gospel for first-century followers of Jesus: they received the gospel at some point in their own past experience, they knew they stood in the gospel every day in their present, and they knew their continued hope for future glory and restored relationship forever. They had a better King, they had a better kingdom, they relied on a better power than any in the world. They knew the gospel changed everything.

The Bible says that the gospel is the good news of Jesus—for eternal life, yes, but also for every part of our life now.

The Bible says that the gospel is the good news of Jesus—for eternal life yes, but also for every part of our life now. So, rather than reduce Jesus' work to one act, we rightly consider how His life, death, resurrection, and reign shape our everyday motives, thoughts, words, and actions. In this, we understand the true biblical gospel, as we seek His kingdom on earth.

A MARGINALIZED TWENTY-FIRST-CENTURY GOSPEL?

If the first-century gospel was expansive, perhaps two thousand years later, "this changes everything" is no longer the common gospel message followers of Jesus always proclaim or hear. The passages above are just a few examples of this: the Ephesians 2:8–9 "saved by grace" passage can be found on coffee mugs, wall hangings, and kids' memory verse cards, but the Ephesians 2:10 "saved for good works" portion is rarely if ever found on products. Second Corinthians 5:17 celebrates being a new creation, but verse 18, that we are now entrusted and sent with "the message of reconciliation," is commonly ignored.

To guard against swinging the pendulum too far, yes, these Scriptures do contain glorious truths about the gospel, which are well worth pondering and praising God for days on end! But it misses the all-inclusive nature of the gospel and its present-day implications that prevailed in the early church. We need a gospel-informed view of the gospel.

Where Our View of God Is Too Small

Based on a new lens—that is, reading the Bible as the story of God, knowing our place in it, and seeing Jesus as the hero—we'll do the hard work of first discovering and then recovering all-too-common areas of life and faith where our view of God is too small, and where Jesus' finished work has been misunderstood, ignored, or minimized. But to do this, we need to embrace what the gospel is: in its past, present, and future aspects.

Christians throw out the phrase "good news" a lot: "The gospel is good news; Jesus is good news." But to keep this phrase from being empty, we play a game sometimes in our church gatherings to see if we know how various aspects of Jesus are specifically "good news." For example, a question I like to ask people regularly is, "What was it about Jesus that made the gospel sound like good news to you?"

I'd ask you, dear reader, to pause and consider your answer to that question now, because there are a thousand subjective ways that God's one objective gospel can sound like good news. Jesus alone is—among a hundred thousand other things—satisfaction to the dissatisfied, joy to the joyless, hope to the hopeless, forgiveness to the indebted, freedom to the enslaved, salvation to those facing judgment, and the answer to every problem. Similarly, there's a reason that every time we see a commercial for diamond jewelry, the stone is set against a black background and slowly rotates as bright lights shine on it. Every slight turn picks up the light differently, reflecting it beautifully. It's one diamond, but each angle shows off its sparkle differently. In this way, the gospel of Jesus Christ is like a diamond. There is one gospel, but there are many angles from which people through history have found that gospel to be truly good news.

> Jesus alone is satisfaction to the dissatisfied, joy to the joyless, and much more. How do we know this? By learning to read the Bible through the lens of the gospel.

The Good News That Is Jesus

How can we discover more and more ways that Jesus is good news? By learning to read the Bible through the lens of the gospel. It's in the pages of the Bible that God shows us many angles of this multifaceted, amazingly precious diamond that is the good news of Jesus. And it's because of those many angles that we can trust that the gospel does indeed apply to every facet of our walk with God, our relationships with others, and our everyday lives. Jesus lived, died, rose, reigns, and will return. Each of those truths is part of the biblical "good news." While no part is complete, each informs the lens through which we read the Bible.

As we learn to rightly read the Bible, and to wrestle with its many passages, we do so not with new eyes, but rather ancient ones. We consider the actual changes Jesus' life, death, resurrection, reign, and return make—both in our reading and in our lives. My deepest prayer as I write is that when you close this book for the last time, you will appreciate God more deeply, will miss the gospel less and instead see how Jesus matters to all of life, and will increasingly celebrate how His truly good news leads us to know, love, and worship Him more.

At the beginning of the chapter, you read, "If Jesus is real, He should matter to all of life." Praise God, Jesus is real! And praise God, His past work that gives us a better hope for our future also informs every moment of our present. It's as we grow in understanding that truth, by the power of God the Spirit, that we rediscover a gospel-centered gospel.

If you're leading a group, see missingthegospel.com for more info on taking your group through the exercises in this chapter.

To Think About and Discuss

1. What was your view of "the gospel"? How was that view formed?

2. What do you now understand the Bible to teach us about the gospel—and its past, present, and future aspects?

3. What was it about Jesus that made the gospel sound like "good news" to you? How is it helpful to see the gospel like a diamond, with various angles and facets of beauty?

4. What are some specific ways Jesus' life, death, resurrection, and reign are each "good news"? How do each of those realities impact and shape our lives? And your life specifically?

5. How will it look to move away from thinking of the gospel only as a key to our eternal life, and to see it increasingly shape every aspect of our current life as well?

6. In what ways do you think you'll need to trust the gospel and rest in God's grace toward you, even as you embody this new truth in your everyday life?

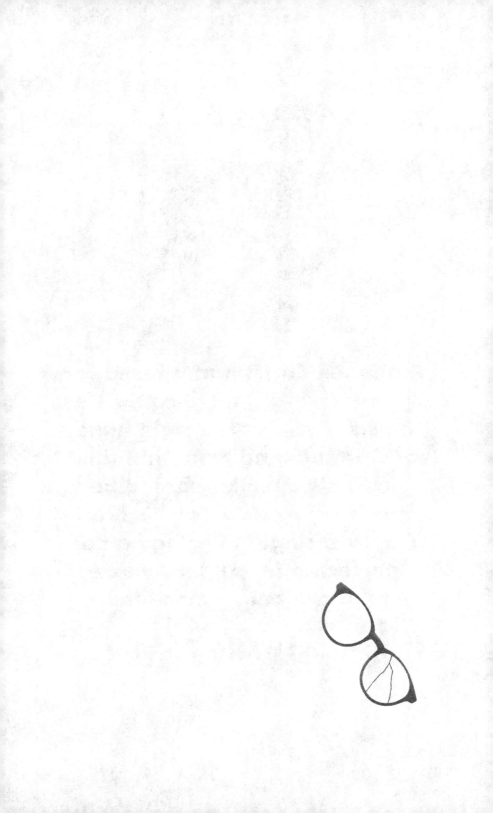

But when Christ had offered for all time a single sacrifice for sins, he sat down at the right hand of God, waiting from that time until his enemies should be made a footstool for his feet. For by a single offering he has perfected for all time those who are being sanctified.

HEBREWS 10:12–14

CHAPTER 5

DON'T
ASK GOD FOR
FORGIVENESS

THE FOG AROUND FORGIVENESS

Kyle was a student in a university ministry I worked for a decade ago. Based on a wrong view of forgiveness, he often dreaded going to bed: what if he died in his sleep, forgetting to ask forgiveness for a specific sin from that day? Similarly, participants of various recovery ministries can be charged to be grossly introspective, always on the hunt for more sin, and then led through somber— sometimes self-flagellating—requests for forgiveness. In my own perfectionistic tendencies, I regularly battle guilt for my sin, which creates a spiral of shame and at times hiding, as I ask God to forgive the same sin over and over again.

Perhaps you resonate with one of these tendencies. Or maybe you doubt your faith's authenticity, feeling that as a follower of Jesus, you should be freer than you are of some brokenness. Maybe you don't merely bring your sin before God asking Him to make you more holy, but rather constantly feel like you have to work your way back into His good graces after discovering *yet another* way you let Him down.

These mindsets do not reflect the true, free, and forgiven life God offers us in Jesus! A disconnect exists between understanding biblically that we have been forgiven and living as God's forgiven people. For many followers of Jesus, forgiveness thus exists in a fog of confusion—and we must clear the fog to rediscover a clear, biblical vision of God's forgiveness.

A deeper issue lies at the source of this confusion: when we live a self-flagellating, penance-consumed, fearful, or continually forgiveness-seeking life, we deny the power of Jesus' work in the cross and resurrection!

ONE WORD, MULTIPLE MEANINGS

A quick "word study" starts to clear the fog and helps us understand a gospel-infused view of forgiveness, because there are different forms of "forgiveness" in the Bible. I've titled and summarized each below, as briefly as possible.

1. **"God's initial forgiveness"** occurs between God and a human, when a human first turns to God, puts his or her trust in Christ as Savior and Lord, and accepts the new, full, free life God offers. In this one-time forgiveness, God (the offended party) absorbs the offense (sin) and frees the offender (human) of his or her debt—one time, forever.

2. **"God's repeated forgiveness"** occurs between God and a human who is already walking with God, for repeated sins he or she commits. Similar to God's initial forgiveness, God frees the offender's debt—but over and over again.

3. **"Human forgiveness"** occurs between two or more humans,

when one sins against another. Whether the offender asks or not, the offended party absorbs the offense and clears the offender's debt. Scripture and our experience both tell us that this can happen over and over, in broken human relationships. For Jesus' followers, forgiving others is based in, and reflects, the greater forgiveness we first received from God, for our own offense against Him.

Before introducing a fourth type of "forgiveness" in the Bible, we must pause.

First, this chapter will put aside "human forgiveness" and focus on God's. Human forgiveness (or the lack thereof) appears throughout the Bible and has been a call to God's people throughout every era of His story. It's important to understand and pursue by the power of the Spirit but is beyond the scope of this chapter.

Second, you likely noticed the repetition in the three types of forgiveness above: each shows an offended party and an offender. In each, the offended party clears the offender's debt. What we haven't seen yet is the means by which that debt is cleared.

Chapter 3 reminded us that the difference between BC and AD is important. As we understand and embrace God's forgiveness, we see one aspect of how important it is.

FORGIVENESS, BC

Sin first entered the world in Genesis 3. God's perfect, unified, worshipful realm (Act 1 of the story, "Creation") became broken by deceit, disobedience, and self-reliance (Act 2, "Rebellion"). As Adam and Eve realized their sin and guilt, they "sewed fig leaves together and made themselves loincloths" (Gen. 3:7). But this couldn't cover their shame or right their wrong. Then, after telling Adam, Eve, and the serpent the consequences of their actions (a microcosm of Act 3, "Promise"), God did what they couldn't do (Act 4, "Redemption"). This redemption occurred through spilling the blood of a living being: "the LORD God made for Adam and for his wife garments of skins and clothed them" (Gen. 3:21). Only the blood of a sacrifice could cover Adam and Eve's transgression.

This began a pattern of sin and forgiveness seen repeatedly in the Hebrew Scriptures: a blood sacrifice was required to atone for one's sin. Sin represented death, and blood represented life. If, as Paul would later summarize, "the wages of sin is death" (Rom. 6:23), then blood—of someone or something—was required, to attain justice and atone the offender's sin. As Nigerian Rev. Dr. Charles S. Allison writes, "It is the life (blood) of the victim that is the source of the atonement, which, of course, brings the hope of the sinner's union with a holy God."[1]

This was not just true for Adam and Eve. Our church once taught the book of Leviticus for several months. (Don't laugh; it was fascinating!) There we see blood sacrifice at the heart of the Hebrew sacrificial system: when one discovered sin (often *daily*), one would bring a living animal to a priest, who—as a mediator—would kill it as an offering, to fulfill justice and restore the offender's standing before God:

> He shall offer a male without blemish. He shall bring it to the entrance of the tent of meeting, that he may be accepted before the LORD. He shall lay his hand on the head of the burnt offering, and it shall be accepted for him to make atonement for him. . . . And the priest shall burn all of it on the altar, as a burnt offering, a food offering with a pleasing aroma to the LORD. (Lev. 1:3–4, 9)

With the offender's laying "his hand on the head of the burnt offering," the animal symbolically absorbed the offender's offense. And by accepting the sacrifice ("a pleasing aroma"), God symbolically restored the offender's right standing (Act 6, "Restoration").

However, *animal* blood was insufficient to cover all *human* sin. Even if one found an animal that was truly "without blemish," it symbolically only covered sins one already committed. So, if the newly cleansed party sinned on the way out from that day's offering, his oneness with God was newly broken, and another sacrifice was required for that new sin.

This act—regularly spilling an animal's blood to cover sin and restore one's standing before God—was the heart of Hebrew worship for centuries. This was "God's repeated forgiveness": God accepted the blood to atone for the offense, and the offender standing before God was restored . . . until he or she sinned again. Repeat, repeat, repeat.

But all that changed in the life, death, resurrection, and reign of Jesus.

FORGIVENESS, AD

Hebrews 10 is the pinnacle of New Testament teaching on Jesus' sacrifice, and on the contrast between old covenant animal sacrifices and Jesus' final sacrifice.

> When *Christ had offered for all time a single sacrifice for sins,* he sat down at the right hand of God, waiting from that time until his enemies should be made a footstool for his feet. *For by a single offering he has perfected for all time those who are being sanctified.* (Heb. 10:12–14)

The "single offering" described here is Jesus' crucifixion: Jesus "has no need, like those high priests, to offer sacrifices daily, first for his own sins and then for those of the people, since *he did this once for all when he offered up himself*" (Heb. 7:27).

In Jesus' life, we see the perfectly obedient, sinless son of God: Jesus was better than any sacrificial animal; He was the full and final "lamb without blemish or spot" (1 Peter 1:19).

In Jesus' death, He also became the full and final sacrifice: He absorbed *all* the offenses God's people committed against God; He was "a single sacrifice for sins" (Heb. 10:12).

Jesus' resurrection proves that God accepted Jesus' perfect sacrifice as sufficient to restore life, and that in Jesus' life after death, death itself (the right punishment for sin) was conquered.

And in Jesus' current and coming reign, we have both a good King who accomplished forgiveness once and for all, and a perfect High Priest who sympathizes with us and mediates for us by His own self-sacrifice and ongoing rule (see for example, Heb. 6:20).

The impact of Jesus' sacrifice—which is one way Jesus fulfilled, not abolished, God's old covenant law and practices—is summarized visually below: both before and after Jesus' time on earth, sin (the offender's offense) removed our right standing before God; both BC and AD, blood was required to absorb the offense and restore that right standing with God. And before Jesus, animal sacrifices repeatedly covered repeated sin—but Jesus' blood covered all sin, once and for all. The fog of forgiveness has cleared: in the gospel, everyone whose faith is in Jesus is already fully forgiven; our standing before God cannot change!

FORGIVENESS, BEFORE AND AFTER JESUS

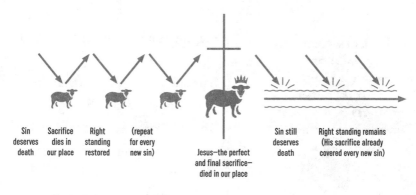

| Sin deserves death | Sacrifice dies in our place | Right standing restored | (repeat for every new sin) | Jesus—the perfect and final sacrifice— died in our place | Sin still deserves death | Right standing remains (His sacrifice already covered every new sin) |

BIBLICAL THEOLOGY VS. RELIGIOUS EXPERIENCE

It may not surprise you at this point in the chapter to learn that God's call to seek His *initial* forgiveness—His single, atoning declaration of our right standing before Him—appears few times in the Old Testament and even in the gospel accounts before Jesus' resurrection, but it appears multiple times in the New Testament after Jesus' resurrection. It's the heart of Peter's Pentecost message ("Repent and be baptized every one of you in the name of Jesus Christ for the forgiveness of your sins," Acts 2:38), and the foundation of Paul's theology and identity ("In him we have redemption through his blood, the forgiveness of our trespasses, according to the riches of his grace," Eph. 1:7). And Hebrews reminds us, "Where there is forgiveness of these, there is no longer any offering for sin" (Heb. 10:18).

It may also not surprise you to learn that God's call to seek His *repeated* forgiveness—His repeated restoration of our right standing, based on our repeated offerings or actions to absorb our repeated sin—is commanded dozens of times in the Old Testament and a few times during Jesus' life before His death and resurrection. Here we can even include Jesus' famous teaching on prayer: "Forgive us our debts" (Matt. 6:12), which fits squarely into Jesus' instruction to a pre-cross Hebrew audience to seek God's forgiveness. Yet the forgiveness they sought would soon be superseded by Jesus' final sacrifice on the cross!

There are *zero* examples or commands to ask God for repeated forgiveness in the New Testament after the resurrection.

But there are *zero* examples or commands to ask God for repeated forgiveness in the New Testament after the resurrection. If Jesus' death covered our sin once and for all, there's no place in post-resurrection life to "ask God's forgiveness" for repeated sins: in Christ they're already forgiven, once and for all.

And yet, if your experience is like mine, there's a tension between biblical understanding and religious practice. I was baptized in the Roman Catholic Church, have attended several services, and took a moving Roman Catholic theology course in seminary. But my primary experience is in mainline and evangelical Protestant churches. Rather than trusting in God's one-time forgiveness in Christ, the charge to "ask God to forgive your sin" resounds in both traditions—even if it looks a little different in each.

On one hand, it's impossible to count the number of times earnest religious pilgrims have uttered the phrase "Forgive me, Father, for I have sinned," not directly to God, but to a priest in a confessional booth. One need not be Roman Catholic to recognize the scene that then unfolds; it's been captured (and stereotyped) in countless movies and literature. The penitent party invites the priest's forgiveness, then lists the ways he or she fell short of God's standard since the last confession. The priest assigns penance—"a prayer, an offering, works of mercy, service, or sacrifice"[2]—and finally absolves the sinner in Christ's name. In short: ask for God's forgiveness through a priest; do what the priest says to receive God's mercy; then your sin is absolved by your actions.

On the other hand, mainline and evangelical Protestant churches don't share the Catholic view that God's forgiveness is mediated through a human priest. But when a follower of Jesus discovers sin in his or her life, the common practice looks fairly similar: in general, if I discover some action, word, or thought that isn't in line with God's— I should ask for God's forgiveness.

But "asking" for something is future-oriented and conditional; it's seeking something I may or may not receive. While in seminary I was first able to articulate a disconnect between two theologies I'd heard: one said I needed to ask God to forgive any sin I discovered. The other (God's New Testament promise) said that Jesus' sacrifice *already* covered every sin I have ever, or will ever, commit.

> If in Christ, God already removed our transgressions, why must we ask Him to forgive us again (and again and again)? If we repeatedly ask God's forgiveness (and carry out penance), don't we revert to a version of the Hebrew sacrificial system?

If in Christ God already removed our transgressions, why must we ask Him to forgive us again (and again and again)? If we repeatedly ask God's forgiveness (and carry out penance), don't we revert to a version of the Hebrew sacrificial system? If God already forgave my sin (through an event that occurred both in history past at the cross, and in my experiential past when I trusted in Him for that forgiveness), why does every Christian tradition—Roman Catholic, mainline Protestant, Western evangelical, and Eastern Orthodox—teach followers of Jesus to ask God's forgiveness anew, every time we discover another sinful act, thought, or desire?

These questions sent me on a journey through the Bible in my seminary days, and I discovered that the common practice of "asking for God's forgiveness" largely stems from misunderstanding two New Testament verses, and a fourth meaning of the word "forgiveness." If we can recover a right view of these verses, the good news of Jesus' life, death, resurrection, and reign becomes all the more glorious as it relates to God's forgiveness!

SAME WORD, DIFFERENT MEANING[3]

In much of the Bible, the word "forgiveness" relates to one's right standing before God—which, as we've seen, occurs through the blood of a sacrifice. In their New Testament letters, however, James and John use the term "forgiveness" differently—and that different meaning is the starting point for our misapplied practice of "asking for forgiveness."

Throughout the centuries, no small amount of confusion has existed between James's and Paul's use of certain words. Reformer Martin Luther even referred to James as an "epistle of straw,"[4] in part because of its use of the term "justification" compared to Paul's. Luther saw James's as "flatly against St. Paul and all the rest of Scripture in ascribing justification to works."[5] In reality, Paul uses "justification" to speak of our right standing before God, while James simply means that our outward actions display (or "justify" or "prove") our inward faith and the change that

Jesus makes in people (James 2:18). In this, James echoes his half-brother Jesus' own words: "The good person out of the good treasure of his heart produces good, and the evil person out of his evil treasure produces evil, for out of the abundance of the heart his mouth speaks" (Luke 6:45)!

Similarly, both James and John use the term "forgiveness" in their letters, and both use it in a way that *seems* conditional and future-oriented—as if God needs to grant repeated forgiveness for repeated sin. But neither writer charges followers of Jesus to *ask* for God's forgiveness, and neither uses the term to refer to our right standing for God. That matters.

James 5:15

The passage in question from James follows the author's instruction for church elders to pray over physically sick church members and anoint them with oil: if the sick party "has committed sins, he *will be* forgiven" (James 5:15). Three clarifications can help us see what James truly means.

First, James's statements are general and about authority. In verse 14, humans can't heal physical needs by *our* power, so we ask God to heal by *His*. Similarly, humans can't forgive sin; we ask God to do so. So there is no guarantee that elders' prayer will produce physical or spiritual healing. Thus, James cares more about human posture than the result: this passage encourages humility (displayed by the sick person's calling others) and reliance (displayed in prayer—which, after all, is inherently an act of reliance on God's power).

Second, in linking physical and spiritual infirmities, James reminds us of the intertwined ways Jesus healed people: physical healing was often a sign of the deeper, spiritual healing people needed. It's right and good, James says, to pay attention to both physical and spiritual needs. While not all physical issues are linked to spiritual issues, James links the two in this case.[6]

Finally, based on the first two clarifications, we see that James's use of "forgiveness" is less about our standing before God (which is how Paul often uses the word), and more about "wholeness" or "restoration": sin can cause physical brokenness, and sin can cause brokenness in our closeness with God. If, through prayer, sin is discovered to cause a physical illness, one's acknowledgment of sin might restore physical health and send the physical infirmity away. And if sin is discovered to cause spiritual distance from God, one's acknowledgment of sin might restore spiritual health to that relationship. James overtly references restoration in the next verse: "Therefore, confess your sins to one another and pray for one another, *that you may be healed*" (v. 16).

James, then, says that if sin causes physical or spiritual brokenness in a believer, God can heal both, and make the person physically or spiritually whole. Even if sin puts distance between a believer and God, we don't need to be "forgiven" again, in the common definition of the term; our right standing is secure in Christ. Rather, we can be relationally restored *by* God, to a fuller intimacy *with* God.

1 John 1:9

John's letter contains the verse that is most used in charging Jesus' followers to ask for God's forgiveness: "If we confess our sins, he is faithful and just to forgive us our sins and to cleanse us from all unrighteousness" (1 John 1:9). First John is also a letter that has been interpreted by various traditions in various ways: once when I was in my twenties, I went to two back-to-back conferences where each used the same verses in 1 John to refute the organization who sponsored the other conference! (*Sigh.*)

It's worth noting that John does not charge readers to ask God's forgiveness for repeated sin. But this verse does read as if God's forgiveness is conditional on our confession.

One legitimate way to interpret the verse lines up with James: confession does not bring about God's "forgiveness" as it relates to our standing with God. Rather, our confession of sin and turning to God is a means by which He restores us to greater intimacy.

A second interpretation stems from seeing that John's letter addresses readers who think they're Christians, but who instead rely on falsehoods—wrong beliefs, their own religious actions, or other forms of morality—as the basis of their faith, instead of true, repentant hearts who hope in Jesus. Of these, John says bluntly that God's "truth is not in [them]" (1 John 2:4).

Growing up in a religious culture, I've seen versions of John's audience my whole life. People think they're "saved" because they go to church; they uphold Judeo-Christian values; they're a little more moral than their neighbor. In this, some religious people falsely believe that this makes them Christians. Their status rests on their actions rather than an actual change of heart, allegiance, and dependence.

Both 1 John 1:8 and 1:10 verify that this is John's audience: "If we claim to be without sin, we deceive ourselves and the truth is not in us. . . . If we claim we have not sinned, we make him out to be a liar and his word is not in us" (1 John 1:8, 10 NIV). Anyone who believes they are sinless is deceived: "The truth is not in" him or her (v. 8); "his word is not in us" (v. 10), John says. In other words, they are not truly a follower of Jesus.

In this second interpretation, John's call in verse 9 is not for believers to repeatedly ask God for forgiveness, but for nonbelievers (who think they are believers) to realize their folly, admit their sin for the first time, repent, and turn to God. Through this lens, 1 John 1:9 is actually about God's *initial* forgiveness.

Whichever interpretation is correct, this verse can't be about Christians asking God's repeated forgiveness. John aligns with the rest of the New Testament: (a) when a nonbeliever initially turns to God, admits he or she is indeed a sinner, and trusts Jesus as their Savior, then God is faithful and just, and *will* (it's a promise, not a hope) forgive their every sin, and purify them from every form of (past, present, and future) unrighteousness, by the blood of His perfect Son; and (b) if our sin distances us relationally from intimacy with God, though our right standing is unchanged, our confession and return is all it takes for God to restore that lost intimacy.

👓 SEEING CLEARLY

As God's people turn from false teaching to God's truth, admit their darkness and receive God's light, and accept Jesus' righteousness for their sin, God's consistent promise is applied: He does forgive—every sin, once and for all. This fuller understanding deeply matters: an "already-and-complete forgiveness" expands our view of the gospel and redefines our relationship with our forgiving God.

To make the point as clearly as possible, then, there are *no* references to Jesus' followers repeatedly asking God for forgiveness after Jesus' life, death, and resurrection. In Christ, you and I are *already* fully accepted by God; we *are already* declared whole and pure in God's eyes. In this truth, Kyle (from the beginning of the chapter) can sleep at night, and those in recovery ministries can stop self-flagellating. We can all be free from our guilt and shame, and rest in a strong assurance, knowing that by *Jesus'* finished work—not by *our* requests or our repeated confessions of sin—we are already, once and for all, fully forgiven and free.

"CONFESSION AND ASSURANCE OF PARDON"

This chapter's final question is, "What do we do with our sin?" Saying that the gospel frees followers of Jesus from repeatedly asking for forgiveness can also sound like an invitation for Christians to minimize our repeated sin. That couldn't be further from the truth.

Rather than a low view of sin, a right view of forgiveness leads us to a high view of God, and a deeper appreciation for Jesus' death and resurrection. While the confessional booth requires penance and repeated forgiveness, several church traditions reflect our right response to ongoing sin: when we discover sin, we participate in "confession and assurance of pardon."

These acts are commanded and practiced by Jesus' followers throughout the New Testament and history: when we discover lingering sin in our lives, the gospel invites and empowers us to confess and repent, and to be assured of our "forgiven" status before God. In other words, in confession and assurance we don't minimize *present* sin; we instead celebrate the magnitude of Jesus' *past* completed work.

First, only if we rest in the gospel will we have the freedom, confidence, and humility to confess ongoing sin we discover—to God and, at times, to others. Hebrews tells us that it's because of the work of Jesus, our Great High Priest, that we can *"with confidence* draw near to the throne of grace" (Heb. 4:16a). Further, when we confess sin knowing we're already forgiven, in the gospel we can be assured that we "receive mercy and find grace to help in time of need" (v. 16b).

As God helps us turn from our sin, we grow a little more into the pure and clean person God already declared us to be. We accept a little more of the gift He gave us two thousand years ago.

Finally, in the gospel, the context of already being forgiven becomes a joyful act of seeking God's help rather than a somber one of fearing His punishment. "God," we might say, "You revealed something in me that is unlike You. But I know it's already forgiven and I'm free—so I want to confess my inadequacy. Resting in Your forgiveness and grace, I need Your help in becoming more like You."

We get to thank God for revealing our inadequacy, and we get to ask for His help in turning *from* our sin *to* a different (better!) thing. And as God helps turn us from sin, we grow a little more into the pure and clean person He already declared us to be. We accept a little more of the gift He gave us two thousand years ago.

The gospel changes our view of forgiveness! Sister or brother, when we discover sin, let's simply confess it to God, ask Him to help us turn our eyes back to Him, and concurrently be assured of God's pardon: in this we get to rejoice. Let's no longer wallow in fear and penance, trying to earn our way into God's graces. Let's stop asking God for forgiveness. Rather, let's rest in the forgiveness He's already granted. And let's celebrate the good news of the gospel, as it applies to our sin: "By his wounds you have been [*truly, fully, for any and every sin, once and for all, already and forever*] healed" (1 Peter 2:24).

To Think About and Discuss

1. What was your view of asking forgiveness for sin? How was that view formed?

2. What do you now understand the Bible to teach us about forgiveness—and also about confession, repentance, and gratitude?

3. What are some ways Jesus' life, death, resurrection, and reign are the starting point for this better view of forgiveness? How does the gospel shape our view?

4. How does it impact you to know the Bible calls us to confess and repent, but also to rest in the promise that we're already forgiven? What response does that lead you to?

5. How will it look to move away from asking forgiveness, while we continue to pursue holiness, confess and repent, and increasingly appreciate Jesus' finished work for us?

6. In what ways do you think you'll need to trust the gospel and rest in God's grace toward you, even as you embody this more-complete truth in your everyday life?

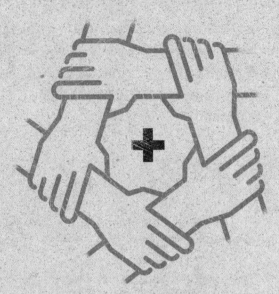

Do you not know that you are God's temple
and that God's Spirit dwells in you?
If anyone destroys God's temple,
God will destroy him.
For God's temple is holy,
and you are that temple.

1 CORINTHIANS 3:16–17

CHAPTER 6

THE
"HOUSE OF
THE LORD"?

THIS IS THE "HOUSE OF THE LORD"?

In 2021, as the world continued to navigate COVID-19, an old theme resurfaced in new worship music. Over the course of that year, many of the most-popular CCM artists released songs that played on radio stations and streaming services, centered on finding joy in, dressing up for, finding healing in, and, especially, coming back to "the house of the Lord."[1] Perhaps it's cynical to think that some songwriters have a similar vested interest as many pastors do: their worth and livelihoods might be intertwined with getting people "back to church" after COVID. But even laying any cynicism aside, it's at least worth considering how much this view of "church" opposes Christian orthodoxy and perpetuates a dangerous view of God, His presence, and our access to Him.

Songs about gathering in God's house long predate 2021. In the mid-1990s, the chorus "come and go with me to my Father's house" filled student camp auditoriums.[2] Similarly, long before

COVID scattered many congregations, song leaders began services by welcoming people "into God's presence," and affirming things like, "It's good to be together in God's house today."

Some churches meet in beautiful cathedrals; others meet in modern concert halls, dark clubs, coffee shops, school auditoriums, theaters, or living rooms.

Some churches own buildings; others rent space—and are often asked when they'll become a "real church" by buying a building. Churches I've helped start have met in pubs, parks, patios and preschools.

In the early days of a church I planted, we met in a comedy club in the heart of our city. In some ways it was a great first meeting space: we loved being downtown; the theater was intimate with seats that sloped upward from the stage, and had 1920s decor, lighting, and velvet seats. But it was dark, dingy, and a little worn and dirty. (There was only one other space in the theater. If the sticky floors in that "kids' room" weren't enough to offend parents, the cigarette butt a toddler once found did the trick.)

One week I was standing in the back of the theater as folks found their seats. That week's guest music leader started strumming with gusto, then exclaimed with a bright smile and hand raised, "We're in the house of the Lord tonight!" I remember specifically watching one young man turn to his wife and grimace, then they chuckled together as they looked at the dark, dingy, dirty theater. The looks on their faces were clear: *This is the house of the Lord?* I smiled at the sight of them and finished their thought in my own mind: *He could do better.*

ENTERING THE PRESENCE OF GOD

A unique doctrine of the Christian faith is that God has always dwelled with His people. He hasn't been secretive about where that dwelling is; in fact, He always invites His people to be with Him, and pursued them to dwell with them. So the principle behind the songs and the leaders' welcome is right: it *is* good to dwell in the presence of God! But knowing where we are in the story of God is vital to understanding God's presence and how we access Him.

At every point in the unfolding story of God, He has regularly dwelled with His people in defined, physical locations. He was with Adam and Eve in the garden of Eden (see Gen. 1–2); as His people wandered the wilderness He led them in pillars of cloud and fire and in the tabernacle they carried with them (Ex. 25:8). Throughout the Hebrew Scriptures, God's presence was manifest in the ark of the covenant (see Ex. 25:22). This was an ornate wood and gold chest, and on its lid were two angels facing each other, each one's wings nearly touching the other's. The ark traveled with Israel in the wilderness and lived in a room called "the Most Holy Place" (often called the holy of holies) in the tabernacle. Then, for nearly a thousand years before Jesus walked the earth, the ark lived in God's most permanent dwelling: the holy of holies, inside the heart of Jerusalem's temple. This room, separated from the rest of the temple (and tabernacle) by a huge, heavy curtain of purple, scarlet, and gold, contained nothing but the beautiful ark, the poles used to carry it, and the stone tablets of the Ten Commandments within it.

For centuries, only Israel's high priest could enter the Most Holy Place, and then only once a year. On the Day of Atonement, after completing a detailed cleansing ritual himself, the high priest entered the sacred space, burned incense, and sprinkled the blood of that year's sacrificial lamb on the mercy seat of the ark. The mercy seat was the space between the angel wings on the ark's lid and was the precise place where God said He met His people (see Lev. 16:2). In this most somber ritual, the high priest would symbolically atone for the previous year's worth of his own sins, as well as all of Israel's sins of the past year.

> If we had lived at any of these points in the Bible, song leaders could rightly have welcomed an assembly to "the house of the Lord."

If we had lived at any of these points in the Bible, song leaders could rightly have welcomed an assembly to "the house of the Lord." Throughout their forty years of wandering, God's people gathered at the tabernacle for worship. Once the Jerusalem temple was built, all of Israel would migrate to the holy site for many holidays and celebrations each year. The Psalms of Ascent, the prayer-songs in Psalms 120–134, are celebrations of Jerusalem, God's holy city, and the temple, the building where God dwelled before Jesus' time on earth. In that phase of God's unfolding story, Psalm 122:1 made sense: since pilgrims would sojourn from across Israel to celebrate God multiple times a year, they could easily sing, "I was glad when they said to me, 'Let us go to the house of the LORD!'" When they arrived at an actual temple with gates and courts, they could rightly exhort each other to "enter his gates with thanksgiving, and his courts with praise!" (Ps. 100:4). This language, and these psalms, are some of the foundations on which many of today's songs and welcomes are built. And while the words themselves are undeniably biblical, we miss, yet again, the fact that Jesus changed everything.

WE ARE NOW GOD'S TEMPLE

Early in my own ministry days, I read 2 Timothy 3:16–17: "All Scripture is breathed out by God and profitable for teaching, for reproof, for correction, and for training in righteousness, that the man of God may be complete, equipped for every good work." These verses are among the more well-known in the Bible— and frankly, are good reminders for the content of this book. But what caught my attention was the chapter and verse where these verses were found: "3:16." I of course knew *John* 3:16. It's the most famous verse in the Bible: "For God so loved the world, that he gave his only Son, that whoever believes in him should not perish but have eternal life."

What if, I naively thought, *by God's providence, every book's "3:16" is the key to life and godliness? Could one verse per book unlock the Bible?* I immediately decided to teach a series on the Bible's 3:16s. (For the record, such a series would 100 percent perpetuate the "little bits" view of the Bible this book is combatting.) I actually came up with a logo, opened a new Word document, and flipped to the front of the Bible to see what every book's "3:16" said. In Genesis 3:16, God tells Eve, "I will surely multiply your pain in childbearing; in pain you shall bring forth children. Your desire shall be contrary to your husband, but he shall rule over you."

I immediately abandoned that idea for a series.

Each book's "3:16" *is* "breathed out by God and profitable." And while reading one after the other won't unlock any magical secret doors, 1 Corinthians 3:16 (and going on to 17) is a "3:16" verse that helps us take another step in recovering the gospel as we read the Bible. Referencing temple imagery, the apostle Paul asks, "Do you not know that *you are God's temple* and that God's Spirit dwells in you? If anyone destroys God's temple, God will destroy him. For God's temple is holy, and *you are that temple.*"

What did Jesus *not* change, as God's story unfolded? God still dwells with His people. God's dwelling place is still physical. And His dwelling place is still holy. What *did* Jesus change?

God's temple is no longer a magnificent building on a mountain in Israel.

God's presence is no longer confined to any single tent, cathedral, sanctuary, auditorium, or building called a "church."

God's dwelling place is now in His people; you and I are God's temple—and even more so, we are God's temple together! That matters: Jesus' life, death, resurrection, and reign changed when, how, and where we engage with God!

GOD'S DWELLING PLACES ON EARTH THROUGHOUT HISTORY

With Adam and Eve, in His perfect earth	In the tabernacle	In the temple(s)	With His people, in Jesus' incarnation	In His people, through His Spirit	With His people, in His renewed heavens and earth

HE'S HERE, HE'S THERE, HE'S EVERYWHERE

At Jesus' final breath, John tells us that Jesus uttered, "It is finished" (John 19:30). Matthew tells us that then, "the curtain of the temple was torn in two, from top to bottom" (Matt. 27:51). In this moment of God miraculously ripping the heavy, thick curtain that separated the Most Holy Place and the ark of the covenant from literally the rest of the world, three things happened: one is often discussed in Christian circles; the other two aren't.

First, as is commonly understood, anyone can now enter God's presence. As Jesus breathed His last and became the full and final sacrifice for sin once and for all, He gave the whole world access to God directly. As we saw in chapter 5, no longer were ongoing sacrifices or penance needed; no more would we need to rely on a high priest or single Day of Atonement to have our sins forgiven. We saw that Jesus is both our final High Priest and our full sacrifice. Anyone in Christ knows that our sins are covered, forever. And anyone on earth can pray directly to God: literally every human is invited to enter the holy presence of God, anywhere they are, however they come, and anytime they wish. He is always ready to welcome us.

Second, but rarely considered, God's presence was released from the holy of holies! As much as the temple curtain symbolically kept people from approaching God, it also symbolically confined God's primary dwelling place to one room. As the curtain tore, not only did Jesus' death let us into God's presence, it also let God's presence out into the world. Some fifty days later the Spirit of God descended like tongues of fire and filled Jesus' first followers (Acts 2:1–4). He indwelled them all, giving each different gifts that would work together to reflect the fullness of Jesus.

The same Spirit of the same God has filled everyone who is redeemed by God and claims Jesus as their Lord ever since. As God the Son died, rose, and ascended to God the Father, God the Spirit now dwells throughout the world, in multitudes of "temples": Jesus' followers. Jesus referenced this reality: "Where two or three are gathered in my name, there am I among them" and that it's to our "advantage that I go away, for if I do not go away, the Helper will not come to you. But if I go, I will send him to you" (Matt. 18:20; John 16:7). John says of Jesus' coming that He "dwelt among us" (John 1:14). The Greek word translated "dwelt" means "tabernacled." He was the fullness of God's presence, embodied on earth. Similarly, if we truly accept that God's people are God's true temple today, God is still "tabernacling" among us; God the Spirit is God's presence, embodied in God's people on earth.

This leads to the third reality: After Jesus' death, Jerusalem's temple would no longer be the place of worship for God's people. As professor Greg Lanier says, "The tearing of the curtain, then, was a prophetic symbol that the earthly temple approached its expiration date."[3] Anyone, anywhere can freely worship God—and that worship can involve multiple activities! And this truth is enriched, as Lanier explains what was done away with:

> The outer *court of Gentiles* was nullified by Jesus's drawing all nations by faith. The *court of women* was nullified by Jesus's making male, female, Jew, and Greek equal heirs of God (Gal. 3:28). And the *priestly courts* were nullified by his consecrating all Christians as a holy priesthood (1 Pet. 2:9). Throughout his ministry, Jesus demolished barriers symbolized in the temple apparatus. The inner curtain was simply the last.
>
> The living God now indwells not a physical structure but the church of men and women from all walks of life, united to Christ who offers unhindered access to divine blessing.[4]

ALL-ACCESS PASS

One of my wife's friends, who did not follow Jesus, went through a really hard time. Knowing I was a pastor, the friend asked Jess,

"Can Ben pray for me on Sunday?" Jess lovingly told her yes, but also explained, "You can also pray to God, Sunday or right now or anytime you want." We may smile consolingly at this request from Jess's friend, but its elements underscore the way even many followers of Jesus still treat our access to God. "Can Ben pray for me . . ." describes a first—even if subconscious—thought: Do we still think we need some high priest to approach God for us, to usher us into His presence?

"On Sunday" describes a second common misunderstanding: Do we believe there is some special access to God that happens on one day (or even, on a few hours on that day), or in a certain building?

Many times, followers of Jesus still see church buildings as proverbial temples. We think there's something unique about those spaces: "church" is where God dwells more, heals more, answers prayers more, or gives us whatever we need (or want) more. I've heard laments from preachers, burdened to bring people "to the throne of God" through their teaching; from song leaders, pressured to make sure the Spirit is "felt enough"; and from liturgists, struggling to "usher people into God's presence" through prayers and readings. If we limit our access to God to a few hours once a week, or to a few specific acts, we strip away the gospel's message and our very understanding of "church."

Jesus was the very presence of God on earth: throughout His life, He was the fullness of God's dwelling (Col. 1:19). At His death, Jesus gave everyone direct access to God and filled the earth with the presence of God. In His resurrection, Jesus was proven the true and better temple, which cannot be destroyed. Since His ascension, Jesus exists with God the Father as our one intercessor and eternal High Priest. Jesus now reigns on earth through His Spirit living in each of His people, through all time and across the world. The gospel gives us a 24/7/365 all-access pass to God. We can dwell in His presence, all day and every day of our lives! After all, Jesus did promise, "I am with you *always*, to the end of the age" (Matt. 28:20).

👓 SEEING CLEARLY

The Bible says that in the gospel, God no longer lives
in a literal temple, but in His people. In this, God invites
anyone to come to Him, and He also pursues us—
whenever, however, and wherever we are. The good news
frees us from limiting "church" to one time or place;
we live as the church together, pursuing mission
and ministry as we dwell in God's presence 24/7!

EVERYDAY CHURCH

If we understand that "you are God's temple and that God's Spirit dwells in you," then our view of *worship* changes: there is something beautiful, deeply meaningful, and irreplaceable about gathering for worship with God's people. But we can glorify God in many ways beyond singing and preaching: "Whether you eat or drink, or whatever you do, do all to the glory of God," Paul exhorts us (1 Cor. 10:31). Or, as Eugene Peterson paraphrases Romans 12:1, "Take your everyday, ordinary life—your sleeping, eating, going-to-work, and walking-around life—and place it before God as an offering" (Rom. 12:1 MSG).

Similarly, our view of *discipleship* changes: we no longer just consider God once a week, but in all of life. There are multiple forms of discipleship that certainly happen as a church family gathers together. But discipleship isn't limited to learning more about God, nor does it stop when we leave a certain building on Sunday. Rather, discipleship becomes a daily pursuit, as we increasingly "love the Lord your God with *all* your heart and with *all* your soul and with *all* your mind and with *all* your strength. . . . [And] love your neighbor as yourself" (Mark 12:30–31).

If we realize we are God's dwelling place in the world, our view of *mission* also changes: rather than inviting people to experience God only in one building, we go into that world, and people around us experience God's presence in and through us. That's being "salt of the earth" and "light of the world" (Matt. 5:13–16; see also Acts 13:47; Eph. 5:8). It's why people can say, "You're the hands and feet of Christ in the world today," or that we're "the only Jesus some people will ever see."

Finally, the fact that we're the new covenant dwelling place of God changes our view of *Christian community*: rather than existing only when several dozen or several hundred acquaintances gather "at church," or even in a designated home for an hour midweek, in embracing the Spirit's indwelling, we necessarily also embrace our need for each other. Chapters like 1 Corinthians 12, Romans 12, and Ephesians 4 explain how God gifted people differently "for building up the body of Christ" (Eph. 4:12). Similarly, there are over a hundred "one another commands" in the New Testament, which help God's people know our role in one another's lives.[5]

Worship, discipleship, mission, and community. These four pillars describe the ministry of most biblical churches. If the gospel changes our view of each, God thus changes our view of "church"! If a "church" building isn't a new covenant version of a temple, and if it isn't an event that happens at a certain time each year or week, what is it? God's "church" is the *people* of God. If each follower of Jesus is a dwelling place of God—His new covenant temple—then another term God uses for His people, collectively, also makes sense: we are the house*hold* of God.

OUR FATHER'S HOUSE*HOLD*

This shift—from church as the "*house* of God" to church as the "house*hold* of God"—seems nuanced, but it makes all the difference in the world.

A house is a *building*; the household is the *people* that "the house holds."

We are God's family, together. Whether gathered in a certain time or place or scattered throughout the week or the world, *we* are God's church. *We* are God's people, who live lives of worship, discipleship, mission, and community every day, because "God's Spirit dwells in you" (1 Cor. 3:16). Follower of Jesus, "God's temple is holy, and you are that temple" (1 Cor. 3:17)!

It's the household—the people—that Paul defines as the true "church of the living God" (1 Tim. 3:15). He reminds Christians in Ephesus that they are "no longer foreigners and strangers, but fellow citizens with God's people and also members of his household" (Eph. 2:19 NIV). God's people, indwelled by God's Spirit, are members of God's household. That's a truer, better picture of "church."

SEEING CLEARLY

No longer do we need to be *welcomed* to "the house
of the Lord"; each Christian *is* the house of the Lord! No
longer do we *go* to church; we *are* the church—
God's household—together. That's why we can live lives
of worship, discipleship, mission, and community,
wherever we are and whatever day of the week.
That's the life the gospel empowers us for,
and that's God's invitation to you.

To Think About and Discuss

1. What was your view of "church" and God's presence?
   How was that view formed?

2. What do you now understand the Bible to teach us about
   church and God's presence?

3. What are some ways Jesus' life, death, resurrection, and
   reign are the starting point for this new view of church and
   God's presence? How does the gospel shape our view?

4. How does it impact you to know the Bible says God invites
   all people to Himself, and also pursues all people—
   whenever, however, and wherever we are?

5. How will it look to *live* as God's church (rather than go to
   a "church"), pursuing worship, discipleship, mission, and
   community as we dwell with Him and others 24/7?

6. In what ways do you think you'll need to trust the gospel and
   rest in God's grace toward you, even as you embody this
   new truth in your everyday life?

"Blessed are the poor in spirit, for theirs is the kingdom of heaven. Blessed are those who mourn, for they shall be comforted. Blessed are the meek, for they shall inherit the earth. Blessed are those who hunger and thirst for righteousness, for they shall be satisfied. Blessed are the merciful, for they shall receive mercy. Blessed are the pure in heart, for they shall see God. Blessed are the peacemakers, for they shall be called sons of God. Blessed are those who are persecuted for righteousness' sake, for theirs is the kingdom of heaven. Blessed are you when others revile you and persecute you and utter all kinds of evil against you falsely on my account. Rejoice and be glad, for your reward is great in heaven, for so they persecuted the prophets who were before you."

MATTHEW 5:3–12

CHAPTER 7

#BLESSED

BLESSED?

"Our new baby. #blessed!" The Instagram caption appeared, but the picture hadn't yet loaded. *I didn't know they were pregnant,* I thought as I waited. In fact, the couple was a little old to have kids. I wondered if they'd committed to foster or adopt. Or maybe they had gotten a dog. I was ready to reply "congratulations!" when the picture finally loaded: it was a brand-new . . . Ferrari: bright orange with black racing stripes. "Our new baby. #blessed!"

What caught me off guard wasn't the high-end vehicle; they're followers of Jesus but did well, and it was within their means. My surprise came from the hashtag: #blessed.

Is that what "blessed" means? Is it a "blessing" to pay a lot of money for a new sports car? Is the blessing that they'd procured enough money to purchase the car—or at least make a down payment—after years of work? *Perhaps,* I thought, *I don't understand what a blessing is.* A hashtag search on Instagram showed that

"#blessed" can mean taking a dream vacation, having a steak and lobster dinner, getting a promotion, winning a junior varsity basketball game, or having a tattoo finished. It apparently also means protection in a gnarly looking car wreck, anniversaries, and welcoming a baby (human, not automotive). And Bible verses are posted online too, reminding friends and followers how #blessed we are. Apparently—perhaps unsurprisingly—*anything* can be a "blessing."

One danger of missing the gospel as we read the Bible is we can either think or we're taught that if we follow Jesus, we're on track to the easy life. There are whole schools of theology that say God's highest goal is to make His people as happy as possible in this life. How does He make us happy? That depends on what happiness looks like to us—or, what we call #blessed. If happiness means being healed from physical or emotional infirmity, that's what God wants, according to this version of faith. If happiness is climbing the corporate ladder, attaining riches, and getting a Ferrari to park in your huge garage, God's job is to pave the way. In this view, we treat God like a clown at a county fair, who exists to give out balloons—in whatever shape, size, and color each child demands. Is that being #blessed?

Of course, you may think, *I'd never treat God like that.* Perhaps not. But there's a subtle version of this too: maybe we don't pursue the lifestyle of the rich and famous but want a life of privacy and comfort. Maybe we don't want the top of the corporate ladder, but rather to maintain our reputation in our upwardly mobile profession. Maybe we simply want to look respectable to our peers, attend a church that regularly adds members and buildings with a smiley preacher who reminds us of God's love, and a community that affirms my personal choices since they're mine to make anyway, all while I pray that God will bless my plans as I put my portion in the plate. Maybe that's being #blessed as a Christian.

Unless it's not.

#CHARMED?

In over twenty years of pastoral ministry, I've had multiple conversations related to guilt and sadness from that view of "blessing." On one hand, if God's purpose is to make me happy—like a clown at a carnival—or even to let me live the way I want, I wouldn't know what to do when something goes wrong. *Does the clown not want to give me balloons anymore? Did I offend Him? Does He not care? Do I need to perform better to earn a balloon?* The pressure to earn God's blessings crushes us. (Besides, "earn blessings" is an ironic phrase.) On the other hand, some things that get called #blessed are thinly veiled versions of how the world defines success or achievement, simply with a Christian spin.

Author and theologian Andy Crouch reflects on this, saying that while we at times call ourselves "blessed," in reality we're experiencing "something much smaller." His word for this is "charmed."

> *Charmed* is a pagan word, a magical word, a word from fairy tales. To be charmed is to be magically held apart from harm, endowed for a time with a bubble of prosperity and power. For one evening, Cinderella is charmed. Aladdin's lamp is charmed, as long as he has wishes left. The sorcerer's apprentice, for a few hours, manages to charm the broom.

> Much of what gets tagged #blessed should be tagged #charmed
> instead. Youth is a charm. Beauty is a charm. . . . There is a slippery
> relationship between being charmed and being blessed, one that
> God's own people seem to struggle to work out.[1]

What if God's highest goal isn't my happiness? What if He has something harder—but better—for me than the easy, comfortable life I want? What if the goal of the church isn't to bring more people in, keep them happy, and have them contribute to bigger buildings, but to form people in Christ over years, challenge misconceptions, and help them rely on God's power over their own—even if our congregation never balloons? What if God gives me finances, not so I can build bigger and bigger barns, but to give away far more than the expected 10 percent to benefit neighbors, needs, and nations? The Bible shows that a truly blessed life is one lived for others—and that starts with rightly understanding our life with God.

BIBLICAL "BLESSINGS": A LIFE FOR OTHERS

Most Old Testament uses of the word "bless," at least in this context, reference God giving some benefit, favor, or power to a person or people—not for themselves, but for His purposes and the benefit of others.[2] For example, God blessed Adam and Eve, then Noah's family, so they could steward the rest of creation and fill it with His image-bearers (Gen. 1:22, 28; 9:1). God told Abram, "I will make of you a great nation, and I will bless you and make your name great, *so that you will be a blessing*" (Gen. 12:2). Abram's wealth, offspring, and notability didn't benefit himself, but others. This opposes today's common definition of "blessing." But it's what it meant to be #blessed: receiving some benefit, favor, or power—but the purpose of God's blessing is to benefit others and serve God. In this context, things like children, reconciled relationships, the Hebrew concept of *shalom* (peace, provision, and welfare), wisdom, and forgiveness are all seen as examples of legitimate bless-ing from God. So perhaps a new Ferrari is less of a blessing from God and more a charm of the world.

> The purpose of God's blessing is to benefit others and serve God.

But a life of service is completely unnatural to us. It has to start some-where deeper: the only right motiva-tion is first understanding our life with God and the true blessings He gives us. Early in the New Testament, we find the Beatitudes. These "blessed are" statements appear in Jesus' Sermon on the Mount and give us a glimpse into how He changes our view of blessing.

I love that *The Oxford English Dictionary* defines "beatitude" as simply "supreme blessedness."[3] In the same chapter as the Be-atitudes, Jesus says He did not "come to abolish the Law or the Prophets . . . but to fulfill them" (Matt. 5:17). It makes sense, then, that He would not only remind His listeners of God's definition of "blessing" in this chapter but live His life as a perfect embodi-ment of the Beatitudes.

Jesus would also later take God's definition of "blessing" to its fullest: if God's blessings always benefitted others and served God, the fullest form of blessing would be literally giving one's life for the sake of God and others. Jesus would embody this greatest blessing in His sacrificial death.

Romans 6:4 says that baptism reminds us of both Jesus' death and His resurrection: "We were buried therefore with him by baptism into death, in order that, just as Christ was raised from the dead by the glory of the Father, we too might walk in newness of life." British minister John Stott sees the Beatitudes in a similar way: "Each step leads to the next and builds on the one that has gone before."[4]

Referring to the image below, I'll summarize the progression as first being emptied (vv. 3–5, like the "death" symbolized in going under the water of baptism), then "hungering and thirsting" (v. 6, admitting our need for Christ alone), and finally being filled (vv. 7–9, like the "resurrection life" symbolized in coming out of the baptismal waters).

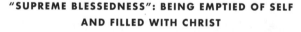

"SUPREME BLESSEDNESS": BEING EMPTIED OF SELF AND FILLED WITH CHRIST

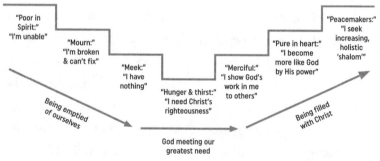

In these ways, we see a relationship between the Beatitudes and Jesus' life, death, and resurrection. We also see a relationship between the Beatitudes and Jesus' current and coming reign: Stott reminds us, "The promises of Jesus in the beatitudes have both a present and a future fulfillment. We enjoy the firstfruits now; the full harvest is yet to come."[5] So when the crowd gathered to hear this sermon, they heard a more complete definition of "being blessed" than they'd ever known—one that was then fully displayed in Jesus' gospel work, which shapes our understanding of being blessed today.

THE BEATITUDES:
RIGHTLY UNDERSTANDING OUR LIFE WITH GOD

1. Being Emptied of Ourselves

The first three Beatitudes are the first steps in Jesus' definition of a truly blessed life.

To be "poor in spirit" means dying to our pride: in a world that says "you can do it" and "try harder," true blessing is actually admitting we're powerless and unable. The blessing in such humility is a reliance on God and His infinite power and ability for literally everything. The only way to enter "the kingdom of heaven" is admitting our inability and accepting God's grace.

"Mourning" is grieving something that isn't right. There's plenty to grieve, inside us and around us. But the Bible defines one source of everything that isn't right: sin and the brokenness it causes. Once we die to pride (Beatitude 1), we can confess sin, rather than hide or downplay it. We can lament brokenness, and concurrently admit we're powerless to fix it. As we turn to God to remedy what we ourselves cannot, we find the truest source of "comfort."

"Meekness" isn't a popular concept. It is admitting that our own strength and abilities aren't enough and humbling ourselves before God and others. If we accept the first two Beatitudes, we realize "meekness" is our right posture before God: we have nothing, but in Christ we have everything! The promise of meekness is that God is a good Father. "The earth is the LORD's, and everything in it" (Ps. 24:1 NIV). When we rely on Him, He provides everything we need in this life, then promises a full inheritance in eternity.

This theme of being emptied fills the pages of the New Testament. Jesus exhorts us, "If anyone would come after me, let him deny himself and take up his cross and follow me" (Matt. 16:24); Paul proclaims, "For his sake I have suffered the loss of all things and count them as rubbish, in order that I may gain Christ" (Phil. 3:8). This isn't how we think of "blessings" today, but it's the first step in a truly #blessed life, according to Jesus.

2. Hungering and Thirsting

Once we're empty, we want to be refilled. In this we have a daily choice: we either choose to be filled with the world's definition of blessing (turning back to the pride, sin, and "self" the first Beatitudes weeded out), or we can be filled with something better: "Blessed are those who hunger and thirst for righteousness, for they shall be satisfied" (Matt. 5:6).

What "blessing" are you hungry for? If you want God to give you your desire, He might do so. He did in Romans 1, and throughout the teacher's life in Ecclesiastes. For a while those "blessings" (charms?) seemed satisfying. But near the end of his life, the teacher in Ecclesiastes realizes the things he thought he wanted—like wealth, women, fame, success, moralism—were meaningless: "I have seen everything that is done under the sun, and behold, all is vanity and a striving after wind" (Eccl. 1:14).

But if we desire God's definition of blessing—when we "seek

first the kingdom of God" and pursue "the righteousness from God that depends on faith" (Matt. 6:33a; Phil. 3:9)—we're truly #blessed. "All these things will be added to" us, and we'll know Jesus "and the power of his resurrection, and [even] share his sufferings, becoming like him in his death" (Matt. 6:33b; Phil. 3:10). Then, we're deeply, eternally "satisfied" (Matt. 5:6b).

3. Being Filled

The next three Beatitudes show what it means to be filled with God's righteousness.

The life and teaching of Jesus are "full of mercy" (James 3:17). He embodies love and compassion. He healed people, cast out demons, told parables about caring for the poor, foreigners, and "unclean"—then actually cared for the poor, foreigners, and "unclean." As we display God's mercy to others, we realize God's mercy to us: whatever state we were in when God found us, He pursued, found, healed, and restored us. "While we were still sinners, Christ died for us" (Rom. 5:8).

"Pure in heart" can't mean 100 percent perfect, always. That descriptor could only apply to Jesus! Rather, God fills us with a love and pursuit of Him, over a love and pursuit of other things. Part of the Spirit's work is removing our impurities and moving us from sinful pursuits toward God and holiness. With rightly focused eyes, we're blessed as we increasingly "see God" and know Him more fully.

The Hebrew word for "peace" means far more than "the absence of violence" or "appeasing others." *Shalom* is all-encompassing renewal and wholeness. "Peacemakers" seek to set the world right, and bring God's kingdom to bear in various situations. This is what

Jesus did as the true Son of God. As we pursue this, we too are "called children of God" (Matt. 5:9 NIV).

Notice, again, that these blessings from God are others-focused: once we're freed from pride, sin, and self—and once we're hungry and thirsty for God's righteousness—He fills us with mercy, purity, and peace. We in turn use His blessings to serve Him and benefit others. This is how Jesus defined and embodied "supreme blessedness." This is a truly #blessed life.

> Once we're hungry and thirsty for God's righteousness, He fills us with mercy, purity, and peace. We in turn use His blessings to serve Him and benefit others.

SEEING CLEARLY

The Bible says that in the gospel, God gave us "every spiritual blessing" (Eph. 1:3). While God defines "blessing" differently than the world does, His blessings are better and eternal. They surpass any circumstance, and this good news frees us from pursuing worldly blessings, and to be generous, bless others, and even suffer for Jesus, who was first generous and suffered for us.

THE SURPRISE BLESSING . . . OF SUFFERING FOR THE GOSPEL

The first seven Beatitudes say we're truly blessed when we die to ourselves, because in this, we become more like Jesus and experience His life, death, resurrection, and reign. Isaiah 53 says Israel's Messiah would come as a "Suffering Servant." Jesus embodied both sides of this title, and when we see "blessing" through the lens of the gospel, we learn that we, like Jesus, will suffer—and that we, like Jesus, can serve others generously.

The final Beatitude shows an aspect of blessing we rarely utter: "Blessed are those who are persecuted for righteousness' sake, for theirs is the kingdom of heaven" (Matt. 5:10). This final promise of this "supreme blessing" feels like the opposite of our definition of "blessing"! To be persecuted, reviled, and falsely accused is a blessing? Because of the world-altering, countercultural life, death, resurrection, and reign of Jesus, God's answer is yes.

If the purpose of God's blessings is to serve God and benefit others, we must acknowledge that history's greatest benefit to others and greatest act of service to God came through history's greatest persecution and most unjust suffering: the crucifixion of Jesus is God's greatest blessing to the whole world. Through this lens Jesus' first followers rejoiced "that they were counted worthy to suffer dishonor for the name" of Jesus (Acts 5:41). In fact, as pastor and author Francis Chan pointed out in a sermon, suffering is mentioned in every New Testament book. He concluded the sermon saying, "It's all over. . . . Someone came up to me after service and said, 'I feel like we just read out of a whole different version of the Bible. I didn't know.' How do we miss these things when it's a major theme of Scripture? As followers of Christ, we'll be hated, we'll be persecuted, but it's worth it."[6]

THE SURPRISE BLESSING . . . OF GOSPEL GENEROSITY

Pastor and author Ray Ortlund helps us see the striking contrast between Jesus' way and the world's way:

If we flip each of the beatitudes to its opposite:

Blessed are the entitled, for they get their way.

Blessed are the carefree, for they are comfortable.

Blessed are the pushy, for they win.

Blessed are the self-righteous, for they need nothing.

Blessed are the vengeful, for they will be feared.

Blessed are those who don't get caught, for they look good.

Blessed are the argumentative, for they get in the last word.

Blessed are the winners, for they get their way.[7]

Our nature and our world both lead us to be number one, no matter what happens to others. Jesus opposed that life, and He calls and empowers us to oppose it too. A servant's role is to be inconvenienced, for the convenience of others. A servant lays down all power and rights and lives generously for someone else's sake. Jesus—the most blessed, most worthy human who ever lived—fought Satan's temptations to worldly power and acclaim (Luke 4:1–12). He instead lived by *God's* definition of blessing and gave Himself to God's purposes.

Before His death, which was the most selfless, generous act of service in history, Jesus pleaded with His Father for His life. But He concluded, "Not my will, but yours, be done" (Luke 22:42). Paul tells us that Jesus "emptied himself, [first] by taking the form of a servant, being born in the likeness of men. And being found in human form, he [second] humbled himself by becoming obedient to the point of death, even death on a cross" (Phil. 2:7–8). In the gospel, we

> **If you find yourself in a time of comfort and peace, enjoy it as God's grace and steward it well. . . . If, however, you're in a season of poverty or suffering, remember Jesus is your Suffering Servant.**

see Jesus' utter selflessness—and we're blessed when Jesus' gospel generosity empowers our own.

For example, if God has given you wealth, it's designed to benefit others and serve God. I forget where I first heard this, but we teach our church that the Bible's view of money is easily summarized as "spend some, save some, and give a lot away." God isn't opposed to some wise saving, nor is He opposed to some enjoyment of life. But Jesus' ultimate generosity to us leads us to be generous toward others (see 2 Cor. 8–9).

Or if you find yourself in a time of comfort and peace, enjoy it as God's grace and steward it well, knowing that circumstances change every day. If, however, you're in a season of poverty or suffering, remember Jesus is your Suffering Servant, who knows your need and wants to bless you richly. In times like these, Jesus invites us to trust God to meet our true needs, and to rejoice that "the sufferings of this present time are not worth comparing with the glory that is to be revealed to us" in eternity (Rom. 8:18). Circumstances come and go. We have good days and bad, ups and downs. In the gospel, God meets us in them all.

The apostle Paul models this mindset, writing to the Philippians that even his imprisonment was a blessing—because God used it for the good of others (see Phil. 1:12–14). He also said the only reason he'd choose to continue living was for others: "To remain in the flesh is more necessary on your account" (Phil. 1:24).

Paul, like Jesus and other disciples, understood God's view of blessing: it's not about amassing wealth, fame, or worldly charms. It's literally *all* about benefiting others and serving God. "I have learned in whatever situation I am to be content," Paul concludes in his letter. "I know how to be brought low, and I know how to abound. In any and every circumstance, I have learned the secret of facing plenty and hunger, abundance and need. I can do all things through him who strengthens me" (Phil. 4:11–13).

Paul understood God's definition of blessing. Jesus was truly blessed. He lived, died, rose, and reigns to truly bless us, as we live in Him by the power of His Spirit. With little or much, in suffering or peace, our lives are #blessed as we're emptied of ourselves, become hungry for Jesus' righteousness, and are filled with the things of God. Whatever blessing God gives us, it's to benefit others and serve God.

In Christ, we, like Abram, are blessed to be a blessing.

To Think About and Discuss

1. What was your definition of "blessings," and what are some examples? How was that view formed?

2. What do you now understand the Bible to teach us about blessings?

3. What are some ways Jesus' life, death, resurrection, and reign are the starting point for this new view of blessings? How does the gospel shape our view?

4. How does it impact you to know the Bible says blessings exist in any circumstance and are given primarily to serve God and benefit others?

5. How will it look to seek God's definition of blessings—and even be generous and suffer for Jesus, who was first generous and suffered for us?

6. In what ways do you think you'll need to trust the gospel and rest in God's grace toward you, even as you embody this new truth in your everyday life?

"Judge not, that you be not judged. For with the judgment you pronounce you will be judged, and with the measure you use it will be measured to you. Why do you see the speck that is in your brother's eye, but do not notice the log that is in your own eye? Or how can you say to your brother, 'Let me take the speck out of your eye,' when there is the log in your own eye? You hypocrite, first take the log out of your own eye, and then you will see clearly to take the speck out of your brother's eye."

MATTHEW 7:1–5

CHAPTER 8

WHO ARE YOU
TO JUDGE ME?

"IS IT A THING? THEN IT'S WRONG."

I don't likely have to remind you of the rampant division across humanity in 2020–21. No matter the topic, our entire society felt caught in a lose-lose situation. Followers of Jesus were just as divided—and seemingly just as hostile!—as those outside of God's family. Divisions raged across the world, perhaps just more overtly than they commonly do, on topics including politics and power, justice, gender, race, public health and safety during the COVID pandemic, and even about what it meant to love God and neighbors in the midst of those divides. Amid all the hurt and pain, I had to chuckle at one meme that jokingly summarized the polarization of that season: "Is it a thing? Then it's wrong."

But 2020–21 was simply an overt microcosm of the divides that separate humans—including followers of Jesus—all the time. Looking back on the divides of that season and people's engagement on all sides of each issue, it's not hard to see three driving factors at work.

First, many people are more than willing to define *the* right answer and to offer that answer to anyone, on every given topic.

Second, many people are increasingly unwilling to listen to another point of view—especially if it's different than theirs, and even if someone has objective or wise authority in a given topic.

Finally, this rejection of anyone else's input, perspective, or *correction* is equally prevalent among God's people. And it's at times supported by a misinterpretation of one of Jesus' best-known commands.

"YOU *CAN'T* JUDGE ME"

"Judge not, lest you be judged" becomes the trump card in many arguments between followers of Christ. Our individualistic lives, love of privacy, and even an unalienable right such as pursuing our own happiness build a threefold wall around our lives, choices, and actions. No one can disagree, offer us advice, or tell us we're wrong, sinful, or unwise. Unless we hold the same perspective they do, their missiles hit our impenetrable defense system.

Think of a time someone challenged your words or action. What was your initial, gut response? Probably not gratitude. "You know, I really appreciate the advice you offered out of nowhere; I think you're right and will gladly change course" isn't our common reply when we feel judged, unless we're being sarcastic. More common is an immediate, defensive, "NO, you're wrong."

Of course, sometimes we *are* wrong—but when we feel judged, our impulse is often to walk away and/or destroy their point. Neither of these actions serves them, or us. Many challenges or questions involve at least something we can learn. Other perspectives grow our wisdom and godliness; after all, Proverbs 11:14 points out that "in an abundance of counselors there is safety." "NO, you're wrong" says the opposite. But in many disagreements, we resort to some version of one phrase: "You can't judge me." Whether out loud or mentally, haven't we all found the log in *their* eye, which to us is always bigger than the speck that might, maybe, possibly exist in our own? Once we decide they're a big, stupid "hypocrite," to use Jesus' word, we negate their ability to point out any speck. (Because, after all, there probably isn't one anyway.)

Perhaps you can't relate to this. But my hunch is that you can. No one likes to be challenged. So, whether your tendency is to fight or fly from conflict, you've likely said or thought a version of "you can't judge me." The fallacy of this thinking runs deep. Ironically, by deciding they're more hypocritical than you are, you've joined them in what initially frustrated you: you're judging them. You assume you're right—or *more* right—than they are.

> **In disallowing any form of judgment— from others or to others—we yet again miss the gospel when reading the Bible.**

But most importantly, if we reject input or advice from others, and even reject judgment from sisters and brothers, we misread and misapply Jesus' command; we miss the freedom and invitation He offers. To reverse the situation, if we don't offer input and advice and even judgment to sisters and brothers, we miss a primary aspect of our shared life and faith.

In disallowing any form of judgment, we yet again miss the gospel when reading the Bible.

"YOU *MUST* JUDGE ME"

Multiple times in the New Testament, God *commands* His people to judge each other! The key to these commands, though, is embodied in Jesus' life, death, resurrection, and reign.

First, Jesus' life embodies the right standard by which we judge—both ourselves and others. The good news of Jesus' life is that He is perfect; He alone 100 percent obeyed God and, indeed, even displayed the fullness of God's character and ways, in every thought, action, motive, and word. In this, the gospel frees us from judging by any other standard and gives us God's.

But knowing that no one could or would ever meet that standard, in Jesus' death God pours out grace on our sin, brokenness, and imperfections. The grace we received from God becomes the motive for our grace we show others in their sin, brokenness, and imperfections.

Then, among other things, Jesus' resurrection reminds us of God's power: if God can conquer death, surely He can change our hearts and the hearts of others in our sin and unwisdom! After all, "If the Spirit of him who raised Jesus from the dead dwells in you, he who raised Christ Jesus from the dead will also give life to your mortal bodies through his Spirit who dwells in you" (Rom. 8:11). While we can judge ourselves and others by God's standard, the resurrection reminds us that only God, by the power of His Spirit, can produce the fruit and change that moves us to that standard.

Similarly, Jesus' reign reminds us that we're not anyone's god, king, queen, or lord: Jesus is! If we trust His reign in our life and the lives of others, we get to humble ourselves and admit our own imperfections. And we relinquish our attempts to control, manipulate, or rule over others in theirs. In other words, the gospel calls us to judge others, but to point them to God's standard and power for change: we judge as imperfect representatives of our one perfect Judge.

Through that gospel lens, let's take a look at some of God's commands to judge each other.

Distinguishing between the sinful acts of people who claim to follow Jesus and those who don't, Paul charges the Corinthians, "What have I to do with judging outsiders? Is it not those inside the church whom you are to judge? God judges those outside" (1 Cor. 5:12–13).

The theme continues, as Paul addresses conflict management between Christians: "Do you not know that we are to judge angels? How much more, then, [shall we judge] matters pertaining to this life!" (1 Cor. 6:3).

Paul even rebukes God's people for *withholding* judgment at times: "I say this to your shame. Can it be that there is no one among you wise enough to settle a dispute between the brothers, but brother goes to law against brother, and that before unbelievers?" (1 Cor. 6:5–6).

Finally, Paul opens himself—an apostle of the Lord Jesus!—to the judgment of others: he charges them to "judge for yourselves" the wisdom and validity of his words (1 Cor. 10:15).

Similarly, even the verses most commonly used to reject others' judgment don't prohibit it. In fact, Jesus specifically charges us *to* judge each other, and helps us know how. "Take the log out of your own eye," Jesus says (Matt. 7:5a). In other words, remember there's a higher standard than your own; test your own motives, thoughts, words, and actions before judging others. But once you've judged yourself by God's standard, "you will see clearly to *take the speck out of your brother's eye"* (v. 5b). By God's standard, judge your brother!

The Bible is clear: God alone will give final judgment of *all people* (see John 12:48; Rom. 2:16, 3:6; 1 Cor. 5:13), and God's judgment alone is 100 percent right, all the time (see Ps. 9:4; John 5:30; Rev. 16:7). But the 1 Corinthians passages are not unique to one city or limited to the first century; they fit a pattern of God throughout history.

> **To rightly understand our role in judging others, we must understand the single standard by which we judge.**

In the Old Testament, Moses appointed leaders, whose charge was to judge "the people at all times. Any hard case they brought to Moses, but any small matter they decided themselves" (Ex. 18:26). Later, God even appointed human *judges*, whose role—in addition to political and military leadership—was determining right action in varied situations. These wise, faithful women and men helped God's people determine right from wrong, good from bad, sin from righteousness, and wisdom from folly, for about four hundred years.

This pattern—God's people offering wisdom and correction to others—continued in the early church. Much of the New Testament itself includes letters, in which servant leaders like Paul, John, and Peter addressed various needs and questions, and also the sin and lack of wisdom in various churches. Reading the Bible is, thus in part, reading a collection of "judgments" on dozens of situations. Jesus' followers are wise to heed these judgments and follow their examples. His followers are also wise to see that every instance of *godly* judgment relies on one standard that's far greater than any human author, character, or person.

To rightly understand our role in judging others, the rest of this chapter first defines the single standard by which we judge, then defines how the Bible shows us different gospel-infused responses for different types of divisions we face.

JESUS IS OUR JUDGE . . . AND SAVIOR

My wife tells me I'd be a good lawyer. This is generally a compliment, but not when we argue. She'd say I've grown over time, but she's right: my tendency is to prove why my point of view is right. "Even when Ben knows he's 98 percent wrong," she sometimes half jokes, "he'll double down on the two percent he thinks he has right, and try to win that two percent." When I do this—and when anyone does something like this—we essentially define right or wrong by our own standard.

But while the Bible makes it shockingly clear that we *must* judge one another, the Bible also makes it clear that the *standard* by which we judge each other is the difference in righteous versus unrighteous judgment. Ungodly judgment starts with our own definitions of good versus bad, wisdom versus folly, sin versus righteousness. It's this judgment the Bible guards against: "Woe to those who are wise in their own eyes, and shrewd in their own sight" (Isa. 5:21; also see Prov. 12:15). This is why Jesus cautions us regarding "the log in your own eye": if we judge anyone by our self-righteous standard of perfection, we set ourselves up for others to judge us by that same standard—and we'll fall short of perfection.

But even when we do this—even as we fall short of the same

standard by which we judge others—we return to the gospel and find even more good news: Jesus took our own judgment, and He pours out grace when we wrongly judge others! The gospel is good news, from every angle: Jesus' life was blameless. He judges others only in line with His Father's judgment (see John 5:30). But His death took God's judgment away from us. "For we must all appear before the judgment seat of Christ, so that each one may receive what is due for what he has done in the body, whether good or evil" (2 Cor. 5:10).

SEEING CLEARLY

The Bible says that in Jesus' perfect life,
God modeled the standard by which we'll be judged.
In His sacrificial death, Jesus took our imperfections,
and we're now covered by His perfection. God's grace
toward us frees us to show grace to others—
but God gives us a standard to judge others by.
We love each other well when we call each other
from sin and toward God!

Outside of Jesus' sacrifice for our sin, being judged by God's standard is terrifying: "All have sinned and fall short of the glory of God" (Rom. 3:23). None but Jesus measures up to God's standard—100 percent perfection. But in Christ alone, we can look to our final judgment with great anticipation, and more fully celebrate Christ's finished work on our behalf: "For our sake [God] made him to be sin who knew no sin, so that in him we might become the righteousness of God" (2 Cor. 5:21). While we all fail to meet God's standard, everyone whose faith is in

Jesus is "justified by his grace as a gift, through the redemption that is in Christ Jesus" (Rom. 3:24). This is, in part, the good news of the gospel: Jesus took our place. He took the judgment we deserve; God only sees us through Jesus' perfect "righteousness"! In the good news of His death, our judge and Savior declares us free of God's judgment.

THE GOSPEL IN OUR DIVISION

In one of Jesus' parables, a king forgives a servant's great debt, but then the servant is unwilling to forgive a fellow servant's much smaller debt. It doesn't end well for the first servant (see Matt. 18:23–35). This is another way the gospel applies to judgment: Jesus' point is that if God forgave our huge debt against Him, ours is to forgive smaller debts against us. But man, that's hard to do when we disagree! The Bible shows three categories of disagreement: sin, folly, and preference. The same gospel that frees us from God's judgment of us also frees us to respond to each category, and to do so differently.

BIBLICAL TYPES OF DIVISION AND RESPONSES

Issues of Preference:	Issues of Unwisdom:	Issues of Sin:
We humbly defer & accept	We humbly warn & discern	We humbly rebuke & discipline

We Judge Sin with Rebuke and Discipline

On one end of the spectrum above, we find sin: sin directly opposes God's commands. As we judge each other based on God's standard, the Bible says a right response to sin is rebuke and discipline from fellow followers of Jesus. From the first sin in history, God judges disobedience to His words and commands. Words like "rebuke" or "reprove" are found over a hundred times in the Bible. And "if your brother sins against you, go and tell him his fault." If he refuses increasing rebuke, eventually the church is to treat the one being rebuked as if he's not a follower of Jesus (see Matt. 18). The goal of discipline is never vengeance, but restoration and forgiveness. For the one being rebuked, the biblical response is confession and repentance. And restoration, forgiveness, confession, and repentance all start with, and point to, the gospel.

We Judge Preference with Humility and Deference

But disagreeing with someone doesn't always mean we can declare them "sinful." Disagreements also occur over preference— the other end of the spectrum above. If the Bible doesn't address an issue, God's grace frees each person to determine their best course of action. And different followers of Jesus engage differently on various preferences. Conflict can arise over things like diet, finances, decisions over disciplining kids or school choice, or ways to engage culture. These are often matters of preference (but might also be "unwisdom," addressed below).

> If God is pleased with us through Jesus, we need not please others: in the gospel, we can shrug, agree to disagree, and let others be in matters of preference.

Paul addresses two matters of preference in Romans 14. Some Roman Christians ate certain meat, which others avoided for religious reasons. Some also set aside certain days for specific forms of worship, while others treated every day the same as they worshiped. Paul addressed both as preferences: rather than divide, he charges, "Let not the one who eats despise the one who abstains, and let not the one who abstains pass judgment on the one who eats, for God has welcomed him" (v. 3). Then he writes, "The one who eats, eats in honor of the Lord, since he gives thanks to God, while the one who abstains, abstains in honor of the Lord and gives thanks to God" (v. 6). God gives freedom, Paul says, so do what you think glorifies God!

If God is pleased with us through Jesus, we need not please others: in the gospel, we can shrug, agree to disagree, and let others be in matters of preference. The gospel response to issues of preference is, "in humility count others more significant than yourselves" (Phil. 2:3). One translation of Ephesians 4:2 is, "Show your love by being tolerant with one another" (GNT). Perhaps that applies here!

We Judge Unwisdom with Warnings and Discernment

One end of the spectrum is sin; the other is preference. Between these exists a huge gray area where disagreement loves to reside: "unwisdom," or folly. Some decisions cannot overtly be labeled sin but are far more important than being preference. These are matters of wisdom or unwisdom. For example, no biblical proverb specifically prohibits someone from walking through the red-light district at night, but Proverbs 7:6–27 warns against the unwisdom therein. A young man lacking in common sense passes the road where there is a woman, "wily of heart" and "dressed as a prostitute." What follows *does* devolve into sin, but the warning itself fits a theme throughout the Bible: wisdom leads to blessing; unwisdom leads to ruin.

Maybe the issue is leaving a church or entering or leaving a dating relationship. Maybe it's a parenting or financial decision that's deeper than preference. Whatever it is, some people don't know what the Bible says about an issue. Others don't know the wisest choice in a situation. Some assume they have freedom if the Bible doesn't *overtly* prohibit something. And some may be blinded to unwisdom in a decision—by their desires or passions, or by forces at work against godliness.

Whatever the reason, Christians judge unwisdom differently than sin or preference. And, since we are called into each other's lives, we often have to guard against the temptation to ignore a hard conversation, falsely treating it as a preference, or condemning it, falsely treating it as sin: we respond with encouragement, exhortation, warnings, and help. Over a hundred "one another commands" exist in the New Testament; by knowing each other's situations, asking questions, and discerning wise courses, we love and serve each other. God's love for us in the gospel drives us to love each other "as yourself" (Mark 12:31). The gospel shapes our motives, words, and actions, so we speak "the truth in love" together (Eph. 4:15). As we submit to Jesus' rule and reign, His Spirit empowers us to care about each other's lives and godliness as much as our own. And as we seek to grow in wisdom, a first step is to intentionally invite it from godly others!

JUDGMENT AND UNITY

Disagreements don't stay "unwise" forever. As we warn and exhort our brothers and sisters—in love and grace—we may understand their motives and actions and discern an issue to be a matter of preference. Or, like the fool in Proverbs 7, unwisdom may lead to sin. In either case, the biblical response changes. But disagreements *will* occur between those who are followers of Jesus. God's church is called to pursue unity. We achieve this not by running from division, conflict, bitterness, or disagreement— for that would be fake! Rather, we seek unity by entering into one another's lives, judging ourselves *and* others by God's standard alone, and displaying and declaring the grace God first showed us in the life, death, resurrection, and reign of Jesus, together. In this, God's Spirit helps us "walk in a manner worthy of the calling to which you have been called, with all humility and gentleness, with patience, bearing with one another in love, eager to maintain the unity of the Spirit in the bond of peace" (Eph. 4:1–3).

Biblical judgment is a loving act that calls people toward God's holiness. In the gospel, we're free to accept different preferences. We warn others against unwise choices. And we judge others too, calling sin "sin," and addressing it humbly and boldly. Because of Jesus' finished work, we can put aside our people-pleasing tendencies, admit our own imperfections, and enter each other's issues. Resting on God's grace, we can "first take the log out of your own eye, and then you will see clearly to take the speck out of your brother's eye" (Matt. 7:5).

To Think About and Discuss

1. What was your view of judging others? How was that view formed?

2. What do you now understand the Bible to teach us about judging others?

3. What are some ways Jesus' perfect life shows God's standard and gives us a standard to judge our own lives and others? How does the gospel shape our view?

4. How does it impact you to know the Bible calls us to judge each other's sin, but also to defer in matters of preference, and be discerning in matters of wisdom? How does the gospel inform each of these responses?

5. How will it look to enter into each other's lives and respond biblically to each of these different forms of disagreement and division?

6. In what ways do you think you'll need to trust the gospel and rest in God's grace toward you, even as you embody this new truth in your everyday life?

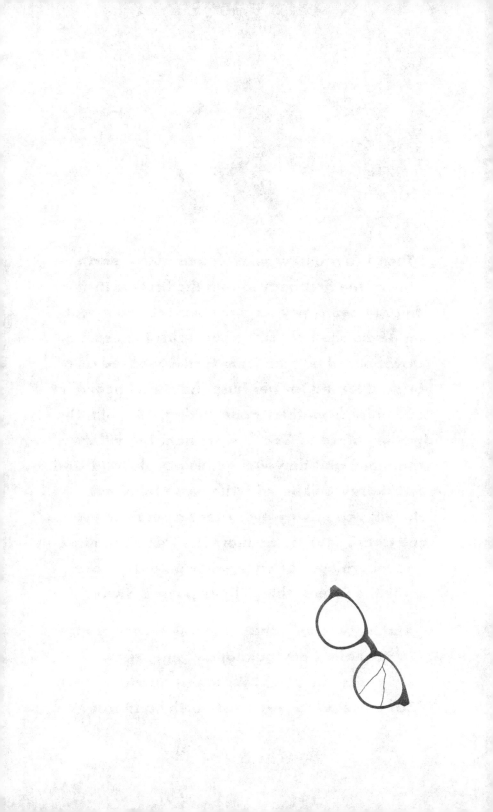

Then I saw a new heaven and a new earth,
for the first heaven and the first earth
had passed away, and the sea was no more.
And I saw the holy city, new Jerusalem, coming
down out of heaven from God, prepared as a
bride adorned for her husband. And I heard a
loud voice from the throne saying, "Behold, the
dwelling place of God is with man. He will dwell
with them, and they will be his people, and God
himself will be with them as their God.
He will wipe away every tear from their eyes,
and death shall be no more, neither shall there
be mourning, nor crying, nor pain anymore,
for the former things have passed away."

And he who was seated on the throne said,
"Behold, I am making all things new."
Also he said, "Write this down,
for these words are trustworthy and true."

REVELATION 21:1–5

CHAPTER 9

HEAVEN IS *NOT* OUR FOREVER HOME

ANTICIPATION REALIZED

In Texas, fall doesn't usually mean *cool* weather, but it feels a little less like the surface of the sun than summer did. This year, however, an early "cold front" (again, relatively speaking) means I'm enjoying the graces of our back porch as I write this chapter: a few leaves on the apple trees in our small yard are yellowing, the dew hasn't yet lifted, and I've traded my Spotify writing playlists for a soundtrack of bird calls and distant traffic. Autumn feels like anticipation realized. The first cool gusts are always a welcome treat after scorching summers. As households with school-aged kids know, the final weeks of summer's anticipation usher in a season when new things arrive.

If any of the four seasons feels like renewal to you, or if you remember the joy of a long-awaited birth or adoption or can simply recall the childlike anticipation of Christmas Eve and the next morning's elation, you know the experience of hope and fulfillment; it's baked into our human experience. On a larger scale, deeper themes of hope and fulfillment have been baked into the lives of God's people for all of history: Israel longed for a Messiah. Jesus' followers long for His return. And Christians set our sights on eternity when we'll be in the presence of our Lord Jesus forever.

But what if our view of eternity is wrong?

What if the common teaching, and thus the common mental images of "our forever home," misunderstands the Bible's teaching on what happens after our death or Jesus' return? And what if the gospel invites us to an even better view than we know, one that makes our eternal lives even more glorious and also impacts our current life today? In this book's final chapter, we see from the Bible that "heaven" is *not* our eternal home, at least not as it's commonly understood. And we also see that this is *really* good news, as we understand the common thread of Jesus' life, death, resurrection, and reign.

The gospel offers us something even better than heaven.

BETTER THAN HEAVEN, WORSE THAN HELL

If I were to ask what happens after Christians die, there's a good chance you'd say something like "We'll go to heaven and be with Jesus forever." Alternatively, some of the most common Christian evangelistic tactics of the late 1900s, early 2000s, and today center on Jesus "saving us from hell." This heaven/hell dichotomy is an easy contrast: one is obviously good, the other beyond bad. Heaven is often pictured as a cloud city in the sky, while common depictions of hell are basically ripped from Dante's *Inferno*: smoldering caves in the middle of the earth. We're told that in heaven we'll worship God forever, so images of winged angels singing songs and playing harps are common in our minds and art; for hell many people picture red, pointy-eared demons torturing deceased humans . . . forever.

The images, language, and contrast in this dichotomy concurrently display the beauty of heaven and scare the hell out of people. But for many Christians, sitting on a cloud forever, singing a millennia-long song, does *not* inspire anything like Christmas-morning anticipation; it sounds better than hell but it's not much to hope for: that version of heaven doesn't sound like a glorious eternity. This tension is actually good because this cloud-sitting isn't what the Bible teaches about eternity. What God actually has planned is far grander than we often hear and think!

ONE DIVIDING LINE, FOR ALL OF HISTORY

The Bible Project's Tim Mackie helps us reframe our thinking, explaining that rather than just saving humans from hell, "the Bible is a story about God wanting to heal His world, and get the hell out of earth."[1] Understanding the Bible's teaching on the afterlife starts with understanding the one divide that makes a difference during this life: one's eternal state is, always has been, and always will be determined by one's faith in God's Messiah. "Messiah" in Hebrew is the word "Christ" in Greek. Both mean "anointed one." To say we put our faith in Jesus Christ is to say we put our faith in God's Anointed One; we say that Jesus is the Messiah.

Christian theology affirms that both before and after Jesus' life, death, and resurrection, God provides one way to be saved and enter into a restored relationship with Him. That single way has always been faith in God's Messiah. For God's people (Israel) who lived before the time of Jesus on earth, salvation was based on what we might call "future hope": they trusted God's promise to send a King, a Savior to restore His people to Himself. For God's people who lived after Jesus' life, death, and resurrection (i.e., Christians, or "the church"), salvation is based on a trust that Jesus was, indeed, God's Messiah; we look back and see Jesus as the fulfillment of God's promise and trust Him as our King and Savior. Whether an old covenant anticipation, or a new covenant confession, "Jesus as Lord," Jesus alone is "the way, and the truth, and the life. No one comes to the Father except through [Him]" (John 14:6).

Echoing the theme of God's presence we saw in chapter 6, Mackie explains, "The overlap of heaven and earth in the Old Testament was the temple [and tabernacle] . . . these temples were decorated with fruit trees, flowers, images of angels, and all kinds of gold and jewels and so on. These were designed to make you feel like you were going back to the garden. . . . Jesus is a temple; He's now the place where heaven and earth overlap." As Jesus spent time with sinners, healing and forgiving them wherever He went, "He's basically creating little pockets of heaven, where people can be in God's presence—but He's doing it out there, in the middle of the world of sin and death. . . . He even told His followers to pray, regularly, for God's kingdom to come, and God's will to be done, here on earth just as it is in heaven."[2]

To understand God's teaching on eternity, we must think of "equal and opposite" directions stemming from this dividing line —one's faith in Jesus the Messiah. There is one path for anyone in history whose hope is in Christ, and an equal and opposite path for anyone in history who doesn't place their hope in Him. This image is a summary of the Bible's teaching in both directions, which are explained below.

THE BIBLE'S TEACHING ON DEATH AND ETERNITY

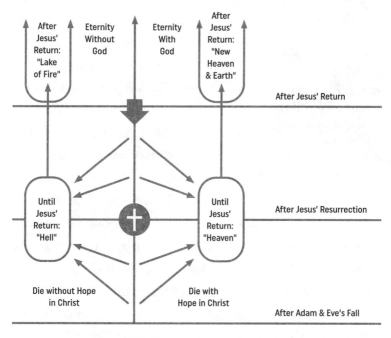

WHERE DO WE GO WHEN WE DIE?

As the image shows, the soul of anyone who dies with their hope in God's Messiah enters a "first stop" of sorts—between their death and Jesus' return, their being or soul is in a state of rest. The Bible doesn't say much about this state, but it's referred to as "paradise" and "Abraham's side" (or "bosom" in some translations) for Israelites (see for example, Luke 23:43 and 16:22, respectively). For Christians, the same state is called "heaven" multiple times in the New Testament (for example, Acts 7:49; Heb. 9:24). So biblically, the Greek word for "heaven" (in this context[3]) is the presence of the Father and where the souls of God's people go when they die—our true "being" is separated from our physical bodies—while we wait for Jesus' return.

While "heaven" is a first stop for the souls of those whose hope is in Christ, an equal and opposite "first stop" exists for those whose hope is *not* in God's Messiah. This other holding ground similarly has various titles in the Bible. *Sheol* is the Hebrew word for "the place of the dead"; the Greek word is *hades* (see for example, Ps. 9:17 and Luke 16:26, respectively). A third term for the same reality is *gehenna*, based on a garbage dump outside Jerusalem. This is where we get the commonly used term "hell" (Mark 9:47). This is the place where the souls of people go when they die if their trust was not in Christ.

> We get glimpses of both heaven and hell during this life as well, in the way people respond to God, in our interactions with one another, and by our relationship with creation and society around us.

Everyone's soul is separated from their body upon death. The Bible teaches that the souls of those who die in Christ find themselves immediately in "heaven," while those whose hope is anywhere but Christ find their souls in "hell." The equal and opposite path is real, but what's often missed is that heaven and hell are both temporary. Our souls don't remain in those states forever, but only until Jesus returns and ushers in a second, eternal reality.

JESUS' RETURN

Books upon books have been written about the return of Jesus. Churches have divided and entire denominations have begun based on different understandings of the hows and whens of His second coming. I will not debate those details here, but we must affirm our belief that Jesus *will* return and that three things will eventually ensue.

1. Every human who has ever lived will be judged. We will be held to one standard: perfection, or sinlessness. Anyone outside of Christ will not measure up, while anyone in Christ will be covered by His own perfection, substituted for our imperfection on the cross (see 2 Cor. 5:21).

2. Jesus will fully, finally defeat Satan, and will remove all sin and evil—including anyone whose judgment deems them imperfect—from His presence as He begins His full reign as King.

3. He will usher in a new reality, "eternity." Eternity looks different for different people, based on the one dividing line: one's hope in Jesus the Messiah.

On these three points, the diverging veins of end-times theology agree, even if they debate the details.[4] While many followers of Jesus are (understandably) confused by the nuances of Jesus' return, this is the point that shows us why "heaven" isn't our forever home and helps us see God's better eternity for those in Christ.

ETERNITY WITHOUT GOD . . .

While "heaven" and "hell" are temporary, the Bible *does* show two locations where all people will exist, forever. These actual locations will host our real, though renewed, physical bodies, which are rejoined with our souls and beings after their temporary "first stop" separations. There's plenty of mystery about how this works, but the Bible's description of our equal and opposite final destinations is clear: those whose hope was outside of Christ before His return will join Satan and his followers in the lake of fire, while those whose hope was in Christ before His return will inhabit the earth—but a perfected, renewed, restored version of earth, similar to how God originally designed creation in Eden.

It's worth noting that this lake of fire was not originally intended for people; rather, Jesus says that "the eternal fire [was] prepared for the devil and his angels" (Matt. 25:41) as a just punishment for their rebellion and rejection of God. God was their good King, but they rejected His reign and put their hope elsewhere. Humans who are sentenced to join Satan and his followers similarly chose to reject God as King and put their hope elsewhere.

While the biblical imagery of the lake of fire is agonizing, it's also fair to see this path as a full extent of God "[giving] them up in the lusts of their hearts . . . to dishonorable passions" (Rom. 1:24, 26). Referencing this reality, Tim Keller writes, "All God does in the end with people is give them what they most want, including freedom from himself. What could be more fair than that?"[5] In other words, those who wanted life without God receive eternity without God. However literal the images of "fire" may be, the greatest agony of an eternity without God *is being fully without God.*

"You make known to me the path of life; in your presence there is fullness of joy," the psalmist writes (Ps. 16:11). Outside God's presence, there is neither joy nor life. Those outside of Christ remain in "hell" until Jesus' return, when He judges them and sentences them to the lake of fire. It's in light of this two-step process that John describes the lake of fire as "the second death" (Rev. 20:14).

. . . OR ETERNITY WITH GOD, *ON EARTH*

Without negating the tragedy, grief, and urgency conjured up by the preceding words, it's the final destination of those who *do* place their hope in Christ where this brief biblical theology draws to a close. God first formed the earth, and everything in it, for

His glory and His purposes. All creation worked in beautiful unity to proclaim the greatness of its Creator and King. Adam and Eve were made in God's image, reflecting His image as they cooperated in His work and cultivated His creation. God walked with Adam and Eve; they enjoyed intimate, ongoing presence with their King. As we saw earlier in the book, this was Act 1 of God's story.

We cannot fathom such a perfect world because it only lasted for a page and a half of our Bibles. Since Genesis 3, God's image has been marred, all creation has become divided, and sin, sadness, brokenness, and death seem to reign (Act 2 of the story). But the Bible teaches that God will do for eternity what He has been doing since Genesis 3: instead of destroying earth, His people, and His creation, God will instead renew and re-create it! Indeed, the apostle Paul tells us that it's not just humans who long to be restored, but that all of creation groans for its own redemption, even as humanity waits for ours (Rom. 8:18–24). Instead of pulling His people to a different planet where we'll watch this one implode, God will restore *this world—our world*—to an even-better-than-Eden state, the likes of which we cannot imagine!

> But the greatest hallmark of this restored earth is the same factor that made Eden what it was: Adam and Eve walked with God on this earth.

"The first heaven and the first earth"—the one that we know, with brokenness, pain, division, and death—"had passed away," John writes in his vision of eternity, "and the sea was no more" (Rev. 21:1). Just as Jesus did with the Old Testament Law, God will complete (or "fulfill") the world He created, not abolish it. In a new era on a renewed earth, "He will wipe away every tear from their eyes, and death shall be no more, neither shall there be mourning, nor crying, nor pain anymore, for the former things have passed away" (Rev. 21:4). Everything broken will be restored. Everything painful will be healed. Everything sad will be redeemed.

No temple will need to exist in the renewed earth, because the whole existence will be filled with God's presence.

But the greatest hallmark of this restored earth—the thing that's better than any gates and jewels of this New Jerusalem, crystal sea, and sinless state—is the same factor that made Eden what it was: as Adam and Eve walked with God on this earth, so will "the dwelling place of God [be] with man. He will dwell with them, and they will be his people, and God himself will be with them as their God" (Rev. 21:3). Indeed, no temple will need to exist in the renewed earth, because the whole existence will be filled with God's presence; neither will there be sun or moon, "for the glory of God gives it light, and its lamp is the Lamb" (Rev. 21:23).

⌍⌍ SEEING CLEARLY

The Bible says that in the gospel, God is "reconcil[ing] to himself *all things*" (Col. 1:20), so that rather than destroying His creation, He will redeem it as our eternal home. This good news for all creation frees us to appreciate all God made and reminds us that God calls us ministers of reconciliation (2 Cor. 5:18): we can steward creation and seek redemption, in all things.

As the greatest agony for those in the lake of fire is being *without* God for eternity, so is the greatest elation for those in the new heavens and new earth, getting to walk in God's full presence— for eternity, in a more glorious version of our own planet than we can fathom!

GOSPEL GLIMPSES OF ETERNITY, NOW

British Columbia is one of the loveliest places I've ever seen. The natural beauty has long captivated this farm boy from flat, hot Texas. This province has mountains, including the best skiing in North America, an ocean, inlets, and temperate rainforests, which I didn't know were even a thing. There's great wildlife, as I can attest having recently ended a hike early after coming across black bear #5! The weather is, I believe, simply described as "un-Texan."

While staying at an Airbnb in Vancouver once, I'm certain I got our hosts in trouble by mixing up the many, *many* rubbish bins. The city had a garbage receptacle, *two separate bins* for types of recycling, and a bag each for compost and paper. It was overwhelming. But it was easy to see why locals here care for the earth so well: there is so much beauty to preserve, protect, and celebrate (or for some, to idolize, as humans are prone to do with any good thing God created).

> **Creation has its own "creation-fall-redemption-restoration" story.**

There are dozens of reasons to form a right theology of eternity. But a primary one is that God's work in this world throughout history gives us a better future to proclaim about the world today than our common teachings on "heaven" and "hell" do. If British Columbia's broken, incomplete version of a beautiful earth gives people a reason to care for God's creation, how much more should a foreknowledge of a fully restored, fulfilled version of earth, which we'll inhabit in God's presence forever, drive followers of Jesus to display glimpses of that promised, coming reality in our lives today?

What are these glimpses of the coming reality we're catching and even displaying? We see these as we interact with one another both in and outside of the church, as we love one another and love our neighbor, as we give a cup of cold water in His name. As He dwells within us and we interact with the society in which He has put us. And as we care for God's creation.

Creation has its own "creation-fall-redemption-restoration" story, and while this may seem unfamiliar and difficult to grasp, there's a similar "gospel story" to the one we know about humans: God created us, we rebelled, Jesus redeems us, and we'll be fully restored. Let me explain. First, "*all things* were made through him, and without him was not any thing made that was made," John tells us (John 1:3). So creation was part of the good work of God, accomplished through Christ. Then, as Paul explains, "the whole creation" is "groaning together" for redemption (Rom. 8:22).

Unlike humankind, creation did not rebel, but creation has been impacted by the coming of sin into the world. Starting in Genesis 3, the very ground is cursed as "thorns and thistles" appear for the first time (Gen. 3:17–19); from that point, all creation has been broken. Just as we in Christ have been redeemed and will be fully restored, not by our own efforts but by God, so also creation will be restored, not by the efforts of Christians (the church), but by God. The liberation resulting from the fall that creation has been "groaning" for will be accomplished by God. "In Christ," Paul writes elsewhere, "God was reconciling *the world* to himself" (2 Cor. 5:19). Finally, we've seen throughout this chapter what happens to earth in the future: God will one day restore His creation; it will become an eternal, perfected version of God's original creation in Genesis 1–2!

MINISTERS OF RECONCILIATION

So there's a "good news story" for humans, and a "good news story" for physical creation. But this chapter doesn't end with a call to environmentalism: that would be too low a motive and too low a bar. Rather, we close with another call: to view all of life through the lens of Jesus' finished work and see how the gospel impacts *every bit* of our lives—because we get to be imperfect ministers of God's "good news story" to everything and everyone around us. Paul describes how the life, death, resurrection, and reign of Jesus gives God's people a new identity:

> If anyone is in Christ, he is a new creation. The old has passed away; behold, the new has come. All this is from God, *who through Christ reconciled us to himself and gave us the ministry of reconciliation*; that is, in Christ God was reconciling the world to himself, not counting their trespasses against them, and *entrusting to us the message of reconciliation*. Therefore, we are ambassadors for Christ, God making his appeal through us. We implore you on behalf of Christ, be reconciled to God. (2 Cor. 5:17–20)

Because of His completed work, you and I are "reconciled to God." Because He makes us like Him, we're given "the ministry of reconciliation"; we're "ambassadors for Christ," sent by a greater King to call people into a relationship with Him. As we live for Him, we represent Him. As we seek to reconcile any brokenness (physical, emotional, relational, and yes, especially spiritual), we bring glimpses of God's perfect future into our imperfect present. We share the story of a better, coming kingdom while we live as ambassadors in proverbial exile here and now. This isn't a new task. Joining God in stewarding God's creation was Adam and Eve's job in Eden (see Gen. 1:28). God has always blessed His people, to bless others (see Gen. 12:2–3). God's people have always been sent to dark places, to "seek the welfare of the city where I have sent you" (Jer. 29:7), through living as good neighbors, cultivating the earth, engaging in commerce, living out our faith publicly, and doing anything else God empowers us to, by His power and for His purposes (see Jer. 29:4–7). But any fruitful reconciliation, of anything on earth, begins with and flows from knowing the depth of first being reconciled to God, through putting our faith in Jesus. Only because we've first been reconciled can we understand God's true heart for reconciliation.

Notice the pattern of God's work: Jesus tells His followers that He did not come to destroy the Old Testament Law; rather, He came to fulfill it. God didn't destroy all people who rebelled against Him; rather, God sought to restore them. Similarly, God will not destroy the earth, but will restore it. God loves His creation, and in the gospel, so must God's people. Jesus entered this broken world He created in order to shine a new light into it, and to restore, redeem, and "unite *all things* in him, things in heaven and things on earth" (Eph. 1:10). Through His redeeming work in our lives, He calls us to "Let your light shine before others, so that they may see your good works and give glory to your Father who is in heaven" (Matt. 5:16). Our charge is to follow Jesus, to face down brokenness—physical, spiritual, relational, or other—like Jesus did, and to bring "the message of reconciliation" to bear. We display and declare the good news of Jesus.

As Tim Mackie puts it, "The union of heaven and earth is what the story of the Bible is all about: how they were once united, then driven apart, and how God is bringing them back together once again."[6] We'll one day see the earth the way God first created it to be, where those in Christ will live forever in the presence of God, who restored us to Himself through Jesus' work and promises a perfected version of this globe where every bit of brokenness is no more.

This is good news! This is the gospel for everything God made! And humans—the pinnacle of creation, God's very image and co-laborers on earth today—get to live every moment of our present lives as glimpses of the future kingdom we, and all creation, yearn for. Because of our eternity here and forever, we live as ministers of reconciliation—and see God's kingdom come, His will being done—here and today.

To Think About and Discuss

1. What has been your view of eternity, heaven, and hell? How was that view formed?

2. What do you now understand the Bible to teach us about eternity, heaven, and hell?

3. What are some ways Jesus' life, death, resurrection, and reign are the starting point for this new view of eternity, heaven, and hell? How does the gospel shape our view?

4. How does it impact you to know the Bible says not just humans, but all creation, follows a "gospel story" (creation-fall-redemption-restoration)?

5. How will it look to embrace your role as a "minister of reconciliation" in the coming days, stewarding creation and seeking redemption in all things?

6. In what ways do you think you'll need to trust the gospel and rest in God's grace toward you, even as you embody this new truth in your everyday life?

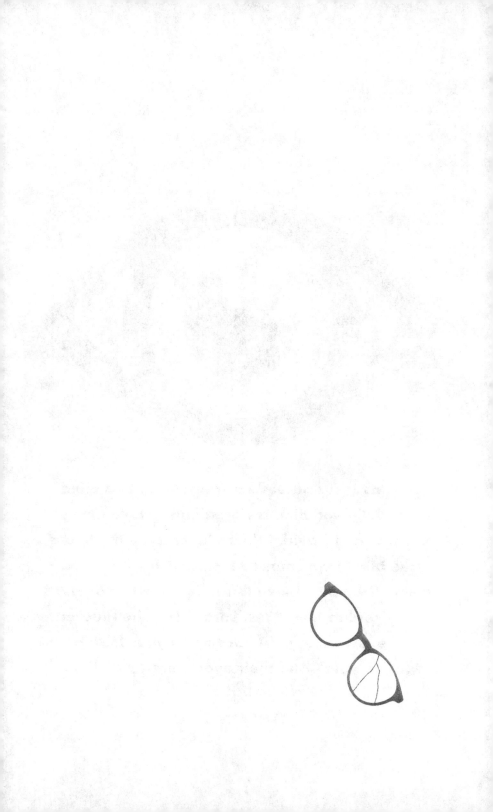

And as Jesus passed on from there, two blind men followed him, crying aloud, "Have mercy on us, Son of David." When he entered the house, the blind men came to him, and Jesus said to them, "Do you believe that I am able to do this?" They said to him, "Yes, Lord." Then he touched their eyes, saying, "According to your faith be it done to you." And their eyes were opened. . . .

MATTHEW 9:27–30

SIGHT
TO THE BLIND

"OCULUS REPARO"

In the movie adaptation of J. K. Rowling's *Harry Potter and the Sorcerer's Stone*, Hermione Granger is the first student to successfully cast a magical spell, repairing Harry's iconic but broken round glasses on the train ride to the students' first year at Hogwarts.[1] It takes only a split second for Harry's old and broken lenses to become "miraculously" fixed—at the hands of an eleven-year-old novice before she even started her formal training in "witchcraft and wizardry"! Following this book's theme, we're something like Harry in the scene: the lenses through which we've come to see the Bible, the world around us, and many aspects of our daily lives are familiar, but broken. It would be great if fixing our lenses were as easy as a fictional movie scene makes it out to be!

But alas, a "quick fix recovery" from the ways we misread the Bible and thus misapply it to our lives is just as false as Rowling's wizarding world. It's also unlikely to be as quick a reversal as my infant son's eye surgery we saw at the start of the book. Rather, as with any bad habit or new way of doing, before us lies a long road of recovery. It's a good road, a needed road, like that of an anticipated road trip. But it's an untraveled road, and there are risks in choosing it. We might be forced from our comfort zones; we might have to reconsider familiar stories and verses. We might need to take more time and pray more as we approach the Bible and consider what it means for our lives.

We might even find ourselves admitting a deep yearning for God and a greater need for Him to show us His truth, as we read the Bible through repaired lenses.

But while hard, all those things are objectively good! At stops along the winding road, and most fully at the end of our journey, we find ourselves at more glorious destinations than any literal road trip. On one hand, through our new lenses we find a deeper understanding of God and His work, and a better grasp of the message of His story, the Bible, and history as well as our place in it. On the other hand, and more importantly, this new lens draws us into deeper appreciation for the magnitude of the finished work of Jesus' life, death, and resurrection, a fuller realization of His present reign and its implications for our walk with God, our relationships with others, our everyday lives, and a better future hope that informs our lives today.

RECOVERY OF SIGHT

This book has been more of a first step of a new journey toward clarity, rather than a single magical spell that fixes every broken lens. We've considered a few Bible verses, commands, and stories, but there are many more to go. Rather than seeing this book as a different point of view to stick on a shelf and forget, view it as an invitation to a new way of relating to God today and throughout our lives. And rather than seeing the end of this book as a final step, I challenge you to take one more tomorrow, then another the next day, as you consider other verses, commands, and stories, asking God to help you see them through this book's new lens. Don't stop at the end of this "postlude"; rather, keep putting one foot in front of the other. "Practice might not make perfect," teachers and coaches remind kids, "but it does make progress."

Some of us may close the book feeling hopeful and ready to continue learning this new lens. Others may feel frustrated or regretful at the ways we've read the Bible before or misapplied it to our lives. Whatever state we're in, in these final pages of the book, the good news of Jesus applies to each of us in the same way it applies to the various verses, commands, and stories we've walked through. Remember that we looked at Jesus' own mission statement when He was in the synagogue reading Isaiah:

> "The Spirit of the Lord is upon me,
>> because he has anointed me
>> to proclaim good news to the poor.
> He has sent me to proclaim liberty to the captives
>> and recovering of sight to the blind,
>> to set at liberty those who are oppressed,
> to proclaim the year of the Lord's favor."
> . . . "Today this Scripture has been fulfilled in your hearing."
> (Luke 4:18–19, 21)

Whatever form of poverty you feel, even if it relates to an inadequacy in your reading of the Bible, Jesus offers "good news";

if some lesser lens for reading the Bible—from personal experience or from tradition—has proverbially held you captive or even been put upon you, Jesus offers you a newfound "liberty." If you're hopeful and excited to take next steps in practicing this new way of reading the Bible, then you can be confident that "the Lord's favor" is upon you because in Christ we have ultimate joy, peace, fulfillment, and restoration. He is the true and best.

But to all of us—no matter our posture or history toward the Bible; no matter how well we do or don't think we know God or how long or short a time we've been following Jesus—He offers us good news as part of His mission statement: Jesus was sent by God, by the power of the Spirit, to proclaim "the recovering of sight to the blind." The theme of blindness was woven throughout Jesus' ministry: during His life, He literally healed multiple blind persons; and He declared woes on spiritually blind leaders— those who supposedly knew the Scriptures but denied Him— calling them (among other less savory names) "blind guides" and "blind fools" (Matt. 15:14; 23:17–19). Some of the earliest celebrations of Jesus were that through Him, "the blind receive their sight and the lame walk, lepers are cleansed and the deaf hear, and the dead are raised up, and the poor have good news preached to them" (Matt. 11:5; also Matt. 9:27–28; 20:29–30; 21:14). Before His own death He was blindfolded and mocked (Luke 22:64), though He was the only human in history who truly saw all of life rightly and clearly. Jesus died so that those spiritually blinded by sin and brokenness could have recovered their sight. He rose and instilled in us a whole new vision for life today, empowered by His Spirit as He reigns now. And He raises our eyes to see something greater than both the best and worst things we'll experience in this life, as we set our sights on the promise of full restoration of all things and dwelling with Him in glory when He returns.

"DO YOU BELIEVE I AM ABLE?"

In this sense, our broken lenses *have already* been fixed—and in a far better way than any fictional teenage witch could dream! Jesus has given us new sight; in Him all blindness is gone, and we have a renewed way to discover Him in His Word, and to see our walk with Him, our relationships with others, and our everyday lives transformed. But as a final word, we must acknowledge the postures that led to Jesus healing some people and His pronouncing woes on others. The difference was whether or not a person admitted their need for His help and sought Him for their healing, or whether they ignored Him, rejected His work, and relied on themselves.

The Pharisees and religious leaders of Jesus' day rested on their own understanding of the Scriptures and their application to life; in claiming sight and life, they were truly blind and dead. The posture of those who followed Jesus during His life—and the posture of those who truly follow Him today—is one of admitting inadequacy, admitting our own blindness, and turning to Him. In this humility and honesty, we find new sight and true life in Jesus. We don't attain either by our own power as we read the Bible and as it shapes our lives, but rather we receive both from Jesus by the power of His Spirit.

This right posture of dependence and reliance on God as we continue this journey of recovery is captured by a final scene from Jesus' life: early in His ministry as He left Capernaum, "two blind men followed him, crying aloud, 'Have mercy on us, Son of

David.' When he entered the house, the blind men came to him, and Jesus said to them, 'Do you believe that I am able to do this?' They said to him, 'Yes, Lord.' Then He touched their eyes, saying, 'According to your faith be it done to you.' And their eyes were opened" (Matt. 9:27–30). The two men knew full well that they could not restore their own sight; they knew that neither their strongest effort, nor any other person, could give them sight. These men's true faith—their wholehearted trust—was solely on the healing power of Jesus, His mercy toward their need, and their belief that He would be able to do this life-giving, sight-restoring work that they couldn't. These men, though physically blind, had spiritual sight: they did not wrongly place their faith, but put it in the one true source of life. And according to their faith, "their eyes were opened."

You and I are like these men: without Jesus, we're blind. And nothing we can do can restore our sight or give us life. But Jesus gives us sight, as He draws our eyes to Him in every Scripture and in every facet of life. I pray that the same gospel that we've considered throughout this book is good news to our own blindness. As we turn our faith to Jesus and declare our need for Him, He gives us sight. He gives us true life, now and forever. He reveals Himself to us in every word of the Bible His Spirit inspired. And He empowers us by that same Spirit to infuse those words into our very lives. The question for us is whether we'll rely on ourselves to read and apply the Bible, or whether we'll turn to Jesus. "Do you believe I am able to do this?" If we answer, "Yes, Lord," then our eyes too will be opened—to life as God intended it to be.

Sister or brother, the gospel *is* the turning point of history. It *is* the one right lens through which to read the Bible and live.

Jesus—in His life, death, resurrection, and reign—*is* the one source of true and full life. Jesus *does* give us the only right lens to recover from all the (shockingly common) ways we get the Bible wrong—ways discussed in this book and beyond. But most of all, the gospel *is* good news—for our past, for our future, and for every facet of our present walk with God, every relationship with others, and every moment of our everyday lives.

> "For from him and through him and to him are all things.
> To him be glory forever. Amen." (Rom. 11:36)

> See missingthegospel.com for exercises and additional resources, to help you keep practicing and going deeper into the chapters and theme of this book.

I charge you in the presence of God
and of Christ Jesus, who is to judge the living
and the dead, and by his appearing
and his kingdom: preach the word;
be ready in season and out of season;
reprove, rebuke, and exhort,
with complete patience and teaching.

2 TIMOTHY 4:1–2

FOR CHURCH
LEADERS

"PREACH THE WORD"

This was the motto at the school where I received ministry training. It was known for its commitment to biblical exegesis and literal interpretation. So, semester after semester, I learned what the actual words on the Bible's pages meant, and how to explain that meaning to others. I was young in my faith and just learning to know and love the Bible during those years. But looking back, I think I learned to preach the Bible's *words*, but not actually preach the *Word*. And there's a difference.

The Bible has two primary meanings of the word *word* as it relates to God's revelation: the Bible speaks of God's spoken *word* and it speaks of God's incarnate *Word*, Jesus. First, throughout history, God reveals His will and ways through spoken *words* (like sayings, decrees, prophecies, His spoken message). *Logos* and *rhéma* are the Greek words in the New Testament for this vital and common definition of "the word of the Lord" (e.g., Matt. 7:24 and John

14:10, respectively). Second, Jesus is God's *Word* made flesh; He is the culmination of God's revelation. The Bible uses *logos* when referring to Jesus as God's Word (e.g., John 1:1; Col. 1:19).

Logos is the most common Greek word for *word* in the New Testament, and is the term used in Paul's exhortation to Timothy to "preach the word." Today *logos* is often interpreted as referring to the Bible: "Preach God's written *word*," we might think. But perhaps shockingly, *logos* is never used in the Bible to refer to the words of the Bible! While God indeed inspired the words of the Bible, and while the whole message of the Bible is God's revealed *word* (His *logos*), if we interpret Paul's charge to his protégé Timothy as "teach people to understand the literal words on the page," we might not actually preach the *Word*, as Paul actually instructed!

PREACHING THE *WORD* FROM THE *WORDS*

"Preach the word," in general, means "preach the whole message of God" (as Paul did in Ephesus: "I did not shrink from declaring to you the whole counsel of God," Acts 20:27). Let us teach the breadth and depth of the good news of God's story; let's share the redemptive work that spans from Genesis to Revelation. But more than that, from whatever passage, theme, verse, command, or story, let us preach God's *truest* "*Word*." Because "preach the word" means, specifically and in context, "preach Jesus"!

Paul's charge follows Jesus' claim that started this book: if true, eternal life is not found in the Scriptures themselves, but in Jesus (John 5:39–40). It's not enough for leaders to exposit a given biblical text and explain its face-value meaning. Rather, we must preach the good news of Jesus—the one biblical message—from every text. Jesus is the culmination of the meaning of every verse, command, and story's meaning. In other words, Paul calls us to preach not just the *words* of Scripture, but the one true *Word* revealed by the *words*. (How's that for a confusing sentence?)

Paul is more explicit in another passage: he tells the Ephesians that Jesus' followers "grow up in every way" into maturity by "speaking the truth in love" (Eph. 4:15). He doesn't mean for us to throw verses at each other or belabor each other with the "shoulds" of God's commands. While the Bible *is* true, we must go beyond "speaking the Bible" to each other. Paul defines the "truth" we must speak a few verses later: "the truth is in Jesus" (Eph. 4:21). It's by knowing Jesus more—His life, death, resurrection, and reign—and by realizing how the good news of His gospel applies to more and more facets of life, that His followers grow in maturity. Jesus is God's truth; Jesus is God's true *Word*. It's Jesus we must preach, to truly "preach the word."

SEEING THROUGH THE WINDSHIELD

Someone has said that the Bible is simply a windshield. Our goal is to look through it to see God clearly. If we become obsessed by the windshield, we miss what really matters. As Jesus charged leaders to see Scripture through a new lens, the fact that God's *Word* is the good news of Jesus—not the *words* of the Bible— changes our focus. We must teach the gospel (the view), and help people see how Jesus' life, death, resurrection, and reign accomplish in us what the Bible itself (the windshield) can't. Here are two examples of how this changes our message:

"Sanctify them in the truth; your word is truth," Jesus prays (John 17:17). While Scripture is true and helpful, only Jesus sanctifies us. This happens as we increasingly rely on Him, as His

Spirit leads us to apply the "truth" of His good news to all of life.

"The word of God is alive and active. Sharper than any double-edged sword, it penetrates even to dividing soul and spirit, joints and marrow; it judges the thoughts and attitudes of the heart," says Hebrews 4:12 (NIV). This verse is often understood to be about the Bible itself, the written revelation of God. But Hebrews 4 as a whole is explaining how God's people enter God's rest: *the Bible* doesn't continue to work so we can rest. *God* does. The next verses clearly show our reliance on Jesus in our weakness: *He* is our high priest; in Him alone we have confidence (Heb. 4:13–16). Only because of Jesus can we rest in God's grace, now and forever.

Consider other terms in Hebrews 4:12. While the Bible shows the *standard* by which God will judge us, Jesus—God's incarnate *Word*—is our only "judge." The Bible can't know our "heart"; it is Jesus who does. "Jesus is alive!" is the resurrection cry of His followers. By His Spirit, Jesus is the "active" presence of God in the world today! Our faith in Jesus as Messiah is humanity's dividing line ("double-edged sword"). This verse is about Jesus and the good news of the gospel, not about Scripture.

We could go on and on, unlearning and relearning what the Bible teaches us about the beauty, vitality, breadth, and depth of God's gospel. How often have we taught people to think *word* (*logos* or *rhéma*) means "Scripture," when in reality, it more often means God's revelation generally—and specifically, "Jesus"? As we saw in chapter 1 of this book, increased engagement with the Bible is vitally important; it's a desperate need for Jesus' followers! But as we recover the Bible's true meaning, we must also point people through the windshield of the Bible's *words*, to the far better view of God's *Word*, for their questions, needs, struggles, and brokenness.

A FULLER GRASP OF THE LEADER'S ROLE

We must also realize "preaching the word" is only one part of a leader's role. The same school where I learned to preach the Bible (but maybe not the gospel) also prioritized the Sunday pulpit as the centerpiece of a church's ministry. Other degrees required fewer hours; any post-graduation ministry job paled in comparison to the role of "preaching pastor" (by whatever title that came).

One phrase church leaders often claim today comes from Acts 6:4: that our primary role is to "devote ourselves to prayer and to the ministry of the word." Devotion to prayer is obviously important. Certainly teaching in the context of a church service or a class is important. And you didn't get this far in the book without catching the message that the layperson should feel confident studying the Bible for him- and herself, something leaders can equip them for. But "the ministry of the word" is not the sum total of leaders' roles, if we believe the Bible's descriptions and commands to "elders," "deacons," and so forth are *all* God-breathed, and still useful today (2 Tim. 3:16). Two clarifications can help us understand this:

First, the verse in Acts 6 was about Jesus' apostles—not local church elders (some served both roles, but here they were functioning in an apostolic task). Thus, on one hand, we must realize that "ministry of the word" was not preparing to teach the Bible to Christians on a Sunday as we tend to apply it today, but being sent to proclaim the gospel in public places where unbelievers could hear in hopes that it would sound like good news they would respond to and be saved (see Rom. 10:13–15). Likewise and on the other hand, the "prayer" in Acts 6:4 is linked to the preaching of the word. It's not referring to one's private devotional time, but public prayer. The apostles approached people—again, often out where people would be and mostly unbelievers—and prayed for their needs and healings. This in turn often led to people declaring faith in Jesus as their Messiah.

This first distinction matters! It leads to a more authentic way to understand the Bible in its right context, and to know what this verse truly means. It also leads to a second distinction: if "prayer and ministry of the word"—rightly understood—was about the work of the apostles, it frees church leaders to seek *all* God calls us to. While prayer and teaching prep are important (and commanded, e.g., James 5:14; 1 Tim. 2:1–2; 2 Tim. 4:1–2 per above), so are shepherding, evangelism, guarding people's lives and godliness, protecting against heresy and false teachers, decision-making and oversight, encouragement, living as an example to others, settling disputes, seeking unity, and equipping the saints (e.g., Acts 20:28–30; 1 Peter 5:1–5; 1 Tim. 3:2–7; 5:17–25; 2 Tim. 4:1–5; 1 Thess. 5:12; Titus 1:9; Eph. 4:3, 12).

Leaders' roles also involve holding to "the trustworthy word" and "truth" (Titus 1:9; 1 Tim. 3:15). As seen above, this means increasingly knowing and dwelling in God's gospel story, seen throughout the Bible's words. And we're to do all this humbly (1 Peter 5:4–5; Heb. 13:17). Those roles are true objectively, in all times and cultures. Each cultural moment, technology advance, specific context, and person in our churches add nuance and more responsibility to this list!

CLOSING GOOD NEWS

Church leadership is multifaceted, complex, and overwhelming. It's too much for any person to do. This is part of why Paul reminds the Ephesian church that in addition to the gift of Jesus' grace (Eph. 4:7), a second gift of God to the church is variously gifted people who work together to "equip the saints for the work of ministry" (4:12). This is good news! No one person can lead God's people or build God's church alone. Only Jesus perfectly fulfills each leadership gift specified in Ephesians 4:11. Only Jesus is the head of the church, who can build His church (Col. 1:18; Matt. 16:18).

When we feel overwhelmed and discouraged, God's encouragement is not what many of us may have heard. Ours is *not* to try harder, trust ourselves, hide our weakness, put on a good face, and get better. Rather, as Paul puts it,

> Such is the confidence that we have through Christ toward God. Not that we are sufficient in ourselves to claim anything as coming from us, but our sufficiency is from God, who has made us sufficient to be ministers of a new covenant, not of the letter but of the Spirit. For the letter kills, but the Spirit gives life.
> (2 Cor. 3:4–6)

The gospel allows us to trust Jesus' sufficiency on our behalf, not to prove our sufficiency. The gospel invites us to *not* base our confidence for the work of ministry in our own education, ability, skill, or experience, but only on God and His work in us. It's the Spirit alone who gives life, not the Law. And these verses don't question whether or not God will be all we need; it's a promise: "God ... *has made us* sufficient"! If we discover that we let someone down, we can rest in His grace and rely on God's perfect presence in their lives. He never fails His people even if we do, and that's good news. If we don't know an answer, we can be free to say, "I don't know"; we can invite them to discover the answer with us, as spiritual siblings on a journey together, rather than pretending we're perfect and know all the answers. God knows all things even when we don't, and that's good news. When someone continues walking in sin and brokenness, we can trust that God has a better Savior than ourselves. Even if they reject our advice, exhortations, and shepherding efforts, we can trust in our one Good Shepherd: God loves them and wants better for them than even we do, and that's good news. When we feel like we fail as ministers, we can receive the Lord's ministry to us, as He reminds us our confidence isn't in ourselves but in Him.

God says elsewhere, "my power is made perfect in weakness"; that truth allows Paul to "boast all the more gladly of my weaknesses, so that the power of Christ may rest upon me" (2 Cor. 12:9). Let's take our calling seriously, and prayerfully and earnestly serve God's people—but let's remember that they're *His* people, who He loves and cares for . . . and so are you. This leads us to rest in God's power and ability in the ministry He alone called and empowers us to, not our own. This leads us to adopt the posture of an under-shepherd and servant, stewarding some of our King's people, trusting Him as the ultimate Shepherd. Jesus called us to the Lord's work; the Spirit helps us do it in the Lord's power.

Sister, brother, and fellow minister, as we recover what God's written *words* truly mean and how they impact our ministry, God's incarnate *Word* incarnate helps us apply His truth—the gospel— to our own lives as well as others'. As we embrace a broader view of leader roles, Jesus—the true head of His church—leads us to trust that His work is better than ours. And as we realize how we come up short in anything we do, His strength is made perfect in our weakness. Jesus makes the burdens of ministry light. His Spirit is our only sufficiency. In God alone does our confidence lie.

Let me close by "preaching the *Word*"—or, applying the gospel—to those of us in ministry who need to hear it: God's work—through Jesus' life, death, resurrection, and reign—is good, freeing news, in each minister's work, and to each minister's heart!

ACKNOWLEDGMENTS

This book, like every book, is the result of many amazing people. Gifted individuals lent some time, effort, thought, creativity, input, and energy to help craft this into the resource it is. I'm beyond grateful to many people, some of whom I likely left out of this list—forgive me!

Amy Simpson and Duane Sherman at Moody walked me through early iterations of this concept, and Pam Pugh is simply the best editor around. (Who knew an editing process could be fun?) Erik Peterson's art may be the best part of the book (ha!). And Connor Sterchi, Jacob Iverson, Jeremy Slager, and others at Moody all lent their passions and skills to help shape this book and its message into its final form. This truly wouldn't have happened without each of you.

Jess, Nicole, Tina, Becky, Kendrick, Matt, and Ben F. all read and refined early drafts—thank you each! Dr. Gerry Breshears helped me nuance some significant portions. And I'm grateful for Don Gates's partnership over multiple writing projects now.

In classrooms or over pints, in one-off conversations or lengthy debates, and in articles and books, I'm grateful that this little book is built on the shoulders of giants. I am hopeful that it adds to the great work of gospel-infused Bible teaching that's come before, and influences that which will come after.

Jess, Char, Mags, and Trav, thank you for sacrificing some family time for this project, and for letting me tell stories about you. It's truly my deepest pleasure on earth to pursue the joy of a gospel-infused life alongside each of you.

Finally, thank *you*, dear reader, for caring about things that matter, for wanting to understand the Bible as God intended, and for dwelling more richly in the good news of Jesus' life, death, resurrection, and reign. It really does matter, to every aspect of our everyday lives!

NOTES

CHAPTER 1—SYMPTOMS: READING THE BIBLE, WRONG

1. Amy Watson, "Bible Readership in the U.S. 2018–2021," Statista, July 22, 2021, https://www.statista.com/statistics/299433/bible-readership-in-the-usa/.

2. Bob Smietana, "Americans Are Fond of the Bible, Don't Actually Read It," Lifeway Research, April 25, 2017, https://lifewayresearch.com/2017/04/25/lifeway-research-americans-are-fond-of-the-bible-dont-actually-read-it/.

3. Stefan Avey, "Visualizing the Catholic Lectionary—Part 1," *Stefantastic* (blog), October 27, 2018, https://www.stefanavey.com/r/2018/10/27/visualizing-the-lectionary-part-1. His article has some helpful and detailed graphics and is based on the work of Dr. Felix Just, S.J., catholic-resources.org/Lectionary/Statistics.htm.

4. Ibid.

5. Joseph Serwach, "Church Every Day: Why 1% of Catholics Feel Called to Daily Mass," Medium, March 21, 2020, https://medium.com/catholic-way-home/church-every-day-why-1-of-catholics-feel-called-to-daily-mass-81a605b21abe.

6. Craig Bartholomew and Michael W. Goheen, *The Drama of Scripture: Finding Our Place in the Biblical Story*, 2nd ed. (Grand Rapids, MI: Baker Academic, 2014), 17.

7. Mike Bird, "N. T. Wright: The Church Continues the Revolution Jesus Started," *Christianity Today*, October 13, 2016, https://www.christianitytoday.com/ct/2016/october-web-only/n-t-wright-jesus-death-does-more-than-just-get-us-into-heav.html.

8. Dane Ortlund, "9 Wrong Ways to Read the Bible (And One Better Way)," Crossway (website), September 30, 2021, https://www.crossway.org/articles/9-wrong-ways-to-read-the-bible-and-one-better-way/.

CHAPTER 2—DIAGNOSIS: MISSING THE GOSPEL

1. Robert H. Thune and Will Walker, *The Gospel-Centered Life* (Greensboro, NC: New Growth Press, 2011), iv.

2. Ibid.

3. "Question 7" and "Question 13," *The New City Catechism for Kids* (Wheaton, IL: Crossway Books, 2018), http://newcitycatechism.com/new-city-catechism/#7, http://newcitycatechism.com/new-city-catechism/#13.

4. Ibid., "Question 15," http://newcitycatechism.com/new-city-catechism/#15.

5. Respectively, 2 Corinthians 13:9; 12:9; Ephesians 3:20; and Luke 18:27.

CHAPTER 3—REMEDY: THE RIGHT LENS FOR OUR EVERYDAY LIVES

1. Craig Bartholomew and Michael W. Goheen, *The Drama of Scripture: Finding Our Place in the Biblical Story*, 2nd ed. (Grand Rapids, MI: Baker Academic, 2014), 17.

2. These summaries are from Chris Gonzalez and Kevin Platt, Missio Dei Communities, https://missiodeicommunities.com/story. Used by permission.

3. Adapted from Jeff Vanderstelt, *Gospel Fluency: Speaking the Truths of Jesus into the Everyday Stuff of Life* (Wheaton, IL: Crossway, 2017), 149.

4. Personal email, February 2022. Used with permission.

5. "What Is Biblical Typology?," Got Questions Ministries, last updated January 4, 2022, https://www.gotquestions.org/typology-biblical.html.

CHAPTER 4—A GOSPEL-CENTERED GOSPEL

1. N. T. Wright, *Paul: A Biography* (San Francisco: HarperOne, 2018), 105.

2. See Matthew 4:23; 9:35; 24:14.

3. Wright, *Paul*, 3.

CHAPTER 5—*DON'T ASK GOD FOR FORGIVENESS*

1. Charles S. Allison, "The Significance of Blood Sacrifice in the Old Testament," *African Research Review* 10, no. 1 (January 2016), 53, https://doi.org/10.4314/afrrev.v10i1.5.

2. "Confession Step by Step," Cathedral of the Blessed Sacrament, accessed April 5, 2022, https://www.altoonacathedral.org/confession-step-by-step/.

3. I'm indebted to Dr. Gerry Breshears, and Moody's editors extraordinaire Pam Pugh and Duane Sherman, for bringing clarity and precision to this section.

4. Martin Luther, *Luther's Works, Volume 35: Word and Sacrament I*, ed. E. Theodore Bachmann (St. Louis: Concordia, 1960), 362.

5. Ibid., 395.

6. In doing so, James echoes verses like Isaiah 33:24.

CHAPTER 6—THE "HOUSE OF THE LORD"?

1. See for example, Hillsong Young & Free, "House of the Lord," or Phil Wickham, "House of the Lord" (different songs); Crowder, "In the House"; Cory Asbury, "Father's House."

2. Audio Adrenaline, "Big House," *Don't Censor Me*, track 5. Universal Music Publishing Group, 1993.

3. Greg Lanier, "Curtain Torn in Two: What Did the Tearing of the Veil Accomplish?," The Gospel Coalition, April 2, 2021, https://www.thegospelcoalition.org/article/veil-torn-jesus-cross/.

4. Ibid., emphasis in original.

5. For more on living out these elements of the Christian life in everyday ways, see *A Field Guide for Genuine Community: 25 Days & 101 Ways to Move from Façade to Family* (Chicago: Moody Publishers, 2021) and *A Field Guide for Everyday Mission: 30 Days and 101 Ways to Demonstrate the Gospel* (Chicago: Moody Publishers, 2014).

CHAPTER 7—#BLESSED

1. Andy Crouch, *The Life We're Looking For: Reclaiming Relationship in a Technological World* (Colorado Springs: Convergent Books/Random House, 2022), 173–74; italics in original.

2. There are other uses of the word "bless/ed" (*bārak*): for example, humans "bless" God; they pronounce "blessings" on each other; etc.

3. *Oxford English Dictionary*, s.v. "beatitude (n.)," accessed April 5, 2022, https://www.lexico.com/definition/beatitude.

4. John Stott, *The Message of the Sermon on the Mount* (Downers Grove, IL: InterVarsity Press, 1978), 46.

5. Ibid., 34–35.

6. Francis Chan, "Is Suffering Optional?," Cornerstone Church, YouTube video, February 22, 2009, https://youtube.com/watch?v=Yghws2fcCt4.

7. Ray Ortlund, *The Gospel: How the Church Portrays the Beauty of Christ* (Wheaton, IL: Crossway, 2014), 71.

CHAPTER 9—HEAVEN IS *NOT* OUR FOREVER HOME

1. Tim Mackie, "Compelled: Speaking and Living the Gospel," Blackhawk Church, video, June 7, 2015, https://www.youtube.com/watch?v=qwNfH_SOWKA .

2. Ibid.

3. The same word, *ouranos*, is also used at times to describe the sky, or the heights above. See "Lexicon: Strong's G3772 *ouranos*," Blue Letter Bible, accessed April 5, 2022, https://www.blueletterbible.org/lexicon/g3772/kjv/tr/0-1/.

4. Interpretations of biblical texts concerning end times/last things abound. My purpose here isn't to debate any of these, one of which concerns the millennial kingdom. The millennium has an important place in the doctrinal statement of Moody Bible Institute, and I want to honor my publisher, while keeping this chapter moving along.

5. Tim Keller, *The Reason for God: Belief in an Age of Skepticism* (New York: Dutton, 2008), 79.

6. Mackie, "Compelled."

POSTLUDE—SIGHT TO THE BLIND

1. Unless, of course, you count Harry's little mishap at the zoo—but in both the book and movie, that incident was unintentional. In the movie, Ron Weasley tries a spell on his rat first, but it doesn't work. And for the record, "oculus reparo" doesn't appear in any of Rowling's books. Hermione is still the first student to cast a spell in the books, but it's "alohomora" in chapter 9 of *Harry Potter and the Sorcerer's Stone*.

MORE FROM BEN CONNELLY

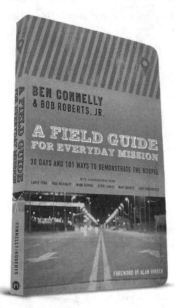

Surprise—if you call yourself a follower of Jesus, He calls you a missionary! You may never go halfway around the world, but because of God's work in you, you are on mission. As everyday missionaries, God has sent us to live out His Great Commission in the ordinary, all-too-busy, and even mundane moments of our lives.

978-0-8024-1200-3

We all know a church is supposed to be a community. In *A Field Guide for Genuine Community*, Ben Connelly shows that the biblical model is the family of God. The church isn't a collection of strangers. God wants you to find a unified, purposeful household where you truly belong.

978-0-8024-2279-8